"As *You Had Me at Woof: How Dogs Taught Me the Secrets of Happiness* attests, you let a dog into your life, he makes his way into your heart. And then you become a dog person. A serious dog person. Though, if you're Julie Klam, 'serious' gets bent into irony, self-deprecation, and outright humor along the way. . . . So what's her gift? Her very appealing personality, which shows up in every line . . . I know that every dog is special and that yours, dog lover, is the most special of them all. But there's something about Julie Klam's dogs and dogs-in-transit that's fun to meet on the page."

—The Huffington Post

"Klam recounts the touching, often hilarious tales of life with Boston terriers. She continues to rescue, foster, and adopt dogs—spirited Hank, adored Moses, chubby Sherlock—each with his or her own special needs, idiosyncrasies, and 'teachable moments' in trusting one's instincts, achieving balance, helping others, finding contentment, loving fiercely, and letting go. This gem of a book is a gift to dog lovers everywhere."

—*Publishers Weekly* (starred review)

"The power of a twenty-five-pound beast to alter a life is made evident in *You Had Me at Woof: How Dogs Taught Me the Secrets of Happiness*. Julie Klam . . . sees her solitary single life turn upside down after she rescues a fugly Boston terrier named Otto, who comes along at just the right time to remedy Klam's status as a commitment-phobe. Klam eventually marries the producer of her VH1 show, a marriage that results in an adorable daughter, Violet, and a parade of foster dogs to and from their tiny apartment after she decides to volunteer for a Boston terrier rescue group. These little one-act adventures in the sacrifices and rewards of dog guardianship have humanity, occasional tragedy and sadness, and plenty of hilarity as this compact family in an even tinier space attempts to save the neurotic, unwanted, and abandoned, including an elderly dog that provides a miracle just when the family least expects it."

—*BookPage*

"[Klam] has a deft comic touch." —*San Francisco Chronicle*

BOOKS BY JULIE KLAM

Please Excuse My Daughter

You Had Me at Woof

Love at First Bark

You Had Me at Woof

How Dogs Taught Me the Secrets of Happiness

Julie Klam

Riverhead Books
New York

RIVERHEAD BOOKS
Published by the Penguin Group
Penguin Group (USA) Inc.
375 Hudson Street, New York, New York 10014, USA
Penguin Group (Canada), 90 Eglinton Avenue East, Suite 700, Toronto, Ontario M4P 2Y3, Canada
(a division of Pearson Penguin Canada Inc.)
Penguin Books Ltd., 80 Strand, London WC2R 0RL, England
Penguin Group Ireland, 25 St. Stephen's Green, Dublin 2, Ireland (a division of Penguin Books Ltd.)
Penguin Group (Australia), 250 Camberwell Road, Camberwell, Victoria 3124, Australia
(a division of Pearson Australia Group Pty. Ltd.)
Penguin Books India Pvt. Ltd., 11 Community Centre, Panchsheel Park, New Delhi—110 017, India
Penguin Group (NZ), 67 Apollo Drive, Rosedale, Auckland 0632, New Zealand
(a division of Pearson New Zealand Ltd.)
Penguin Books (South Africa) (Pty.) Ltd., 24 Sturdee Avenue, Rosebank, Johannesburg 2196, South Africa

Penguin Books Ltd., Registered Offices: 80 Strand, London WC2R 0RL, England

Cover design by Abby Weintraub
Book design by Meighan Cavanaugh

First Riverhead hardcover edition: October 2010
First Riverhead trade paperback edition: October 2011
Riverhead trade paperback ISBN: 978-1-59448-541-1

The Library of Congress has catalogued the Riverhead hardcover edition as follows:

Klam, Julie.
You had me at woof : how dogs taught me the secrets of happiness / Julie Klam
p. cm.
ISBN 978-1-59448-776-7
1. Klam, Julie. 2. Dogs—Therapeutic use. 3. Dog owners—Biography. 4. Human-animal relationships. I. Title.
RM931.D63K53 2010 2010004942
615.8'5158—dc22

PRINTED IN THE UNITED STATES OF AMERICA

10 9 8 7 6 5 4 3 2 1

Penguin is committed to publishing works of quality and integrity.
In that spirit, we are proud to offer this book to our readers;
however, the story, the experiences, and the words
are the author's alone.

For Paul,

who has never said no

to a dog who needs us

Contents

LESSON ONE

How to Find the Right One for You 1

LESSON TWO

How to Find the Parachute Color That's Most Flattering to You 21

LESSON THREE

How to Keep the Yin from Strangling the Yang 35

LESSON FOUR

How to Listen to That Still, Small Voice 55

LESSON FIVE

How to Be an Amateur Therapist 75

LESSON SIX

How to Fall in Love . . . Again 97

LESSON SEVEN

How to Mourn the Loss of a Friend 119

LESSON EIGHT

How to Uncover Truths 131

LESSON NINE

How to Feel Good About Your Neck 157

LESSON TEN

How to Find Happiness 179

LESSON ELEVEN

How to Find the Right Fit 213

Acknowledgments 227

"The humans have tried everything. Now it's up to us dogs!"

—Danny, *101 Dalmatians*

LESSON ONE

How to Find the Right One for You

One night I dreamed I had a dog. He was a Boston terrier, not stocky, but substantial, with a good face. He came slow-motion scampering through the high grass and wild daisies of my sleep. He was perfect in every way, and I instantly felt an unexplainable future love for him, the kind I'd always imagined I'd feel when I met my soul mate—the Sonny to my Cher. His eyes were big O's and it looked like his face was spelling O-T-T-O, so I knew that had to be his name, and that I had to go find him.

I was thirty, living alone in Manhattan, and employed part-time as a clerk in an insurance company. The only thing I felt sure of was that I wasn't where I was supposed to be.

With no career and no boyfriend, I had the feeling that I was waiting for my life to start, and I needed something special to show me how to make it happen.

I believed everything was a sign. I went to my parents' house and found a *Close Encounters of the Third Kind* T-shirt in the attic that I'd never seen before and thought, Maybe I'm going to work with Steven Spielberg . . . or be contacted by aliens; or I'd buy a pair of pants and find a square of paper in the pocket that said "INSPECTED BY 34," and think, I'll meet my husband when I'm thirty-four, or, I need to lose thirty-four pounds.

After the Otto dream, I called my friend Barbara at work because I knew she'd understand. We were both going through a period of fogginess in our lives and were looking for clarity, which we chose to seek in the reliable forms of psychics, seers, tarot card readers, crystal goddesses, and astrologers. We were certain that definitive answers—perhaps in the guise of a nice Michelin road map—were laid out somewhere. All we wanted was to know what was going to happen so we could stop worrying about it. Was that so much to ask? We just needed names, dates, and locations. My mother, who worked as a healer, had a steady stream of recommendations, though she always emphasized our lives were ours to do with what we wanted. But we didn't know what we wanted. We wanted someone to tell us.

I'd call my mom up and say, "Bad news, I'm not going to meet my husband for five years. I might as well just stay home and watch TV."

"No," she explained, "you are in charge of your own path. All of the great yogis say you have free will; these are just suggestions of what may happen if you do nothing."

"Oh good, so I won't necessarily die in a hang-gliding accident?"

"Why would you be hang gliding? You're definitely not going to die hang gliding because you won't be going hang gliding! What are you, Bruce Willis?" Even though she was a healer, she was a Jewish mother first.

But this Otto dream seemed significant and I wanted Barbara's take.

"Is that the kind of dog that looks like a cat?"

"Yes," I said, "kind of like a cat and an old man combined."

"Oh, I think that's the kind of dog Michael has." She held her hand over the mouthpiece and asked Michael, her funny, gay coworker, if Buster was a Boston terrier. I heard him say yes and start espousing his virtues. Then she asked me if I wanted to know where he got it.

"Sure," I said and waited while she got the breeder's name and number, thinking that this all figured into the magic; I mean, what were the chances that a guy who worked in Barbara's office had the very same kind of dog I dreamed about?

I did some research on Boston terriers to see if they'd work as an apartment dog and what their shedding ratio was. I was in luck: in the book *Finding the Breed That's Right for You*, Bostons got five out of five stars in the categories of apartment suitability and hypoallergenicity.

I found out that the Boston terrier originated when an English bulldog and an English terrier were bred and then the product was bred with a bulldog. Though they were not intentionally bred for it, Bostons have a very pronounced loyalty to their masters. Because they looked like they were wearing tuxedos, they were nicknamed the "American Gentleman." Though I'm not the formal type, their look was very appealing to me. I'd seen them in early silent films and they felt old-fashioned and classic. They were kind of like Harold Lloyd as dog. And they were very popular around New York City during my grandparents' childhood, which made them even more comforting to me.

A few days later, armed with my vast knowledge of Bostons, I gave the breeder a call. "We're not doing Boston puppies anytime soon, we're concentrating on Frenchies," she said, referring to the Boston's "cousin," the French bulldog. "But we're involved with Boston terrier rescue. Do you know what that is?" I said yes even though I didn't. I sort of figured it had to do with rescuing Boston terriers in peril. You know, stuck up in trees, stranded on ice floes.

"We're fostering a young male, about a year and a half, and the people who were supposed to take him never showed up." She said he'd been on the street for a long time when he was brought into the shelter in the winter; he still had summer fleas, and mange, and was skin and bones. They were nursing him back to health, and with all he'd been through, he'd never, not once, had an accident in the house. "He really is a wonderful dog," she said, adding, "All he really needs is a little love," which made me imagine the dog version of the Charlie Brown Christmas tree. "We've been calling him Buddy. His ears droop over; he's definitely not show quality, but if you don't care about that, then he's perfect." While I talked to her I wrote down on a piece of paper "ears," "show quality," and "Buddy." I don't know if I shouted, *"I'll take him!"* or if it just felt like that. It turned out the people who stood him up the day before called a few minutes after me but the breeder said it was too late. Another girl was coming to get him. Me.

He was way out in Pennsylvania, though, and I had to get someone to drive me there.

When I hung up I said, *"Am I getting a dog?"*

I was convinced that doing anything to shake up my world would help with the at-sea feeling permeating every aspect of my life. I really wanted to meet a guy, and all of the conventional ways, like hanging out in bookstores and coffee bars and taking classes in biodiversity at the American Museum of Natural History and, the one I did most, sitting in my apartment watching TV, weren't working. I needed to find something to get me out and about that wasn't so contrived. I'd grown up with dogs, but they were huge English mastiffs that I was terribly allergic to. I liked them as much as you can like anyone whose mere presence gives you an acute asthma attack. Recently I had started looking into the hypoallergenic breeds. Apparently poodles were fine, but I wasn't crazy about them despite the claims that they are the smartest breed of dog. (I never understood how that was determined. Were they found by their owners hooking up Bunsen burners and pouring liquids into flasks?) I believe that different dog breeds speak to different people. The first time I'd seen a Boston was in a black-and-white photo with the actor/comedian Chris Elliott that hung in his foyer. I babysat for his kids and when they were asleep, I stared at the photo, captivated. When I asked Chris about it, he said the dog was just a prop for the photo shoot, but he remembered he was cute as a button. As loopy as it may sound, every time since then that I passed a Boston terrier on the street, I felt a little tug, a small flat-faced voice saying to me, "You and I should be together."

Once the decision was made to get "Buddy," I started, like any mother-to-be, to purchase things. This was where I could really bring my expertise as a shopper to bear. I bought a red-and-black-checked dog bed from Orvis and in a trimming store I found small varsity football letters. I bought two sets of Offensive Tackle letters and sewed "O-T-T-O" onto the front of the bed. I sent away for an engraved name tag in the shape of a bone, and spent hours poring over the contents of dog catalogs, putting check marks next to bowls, revolting-sounding treats like pig ears and marrow bones, stuffed animals that had squeakers, Kong toys, Nylabones, collars, and leashes in a variety of colors and patterns. I bought four books, all called *Boston Terrier*. In short, I went nuts.

The night before my aunt Mattie and I went to get him I stood in the kitchen of my small studio looking at his bed with all of the toys lined up neatly beside it, a few treats on the pillow. "Tomorrow at this time, a real live dog will be in that bed." I could hardly sleep that night.

It was an awful, nasty, sleety March day when we drove to the rural Pennsylvania county where the breeder lived. On the way, I began to get nervous, really nervous.

"What's wrong?" Mattie said to me, looking over from the driver's seat. Her own dog, Harry, a mutt she rescued from the side of the Bronx River Parkway going north, was sitting on her lap. "Your lips are white."

"Nothing."

"You don't have to do this," she said. "We can turn right around."

"I want to."

Mattie was a wonderful aunt, but at this moment her concern was not for me. What troubled Mattie, the most insane dog person I or anyone else had known, a woman who ordered room service entrees of filet mignon for her pups, was that I'd get this dog and not treat it well and then she'd stop liking me.

Picking Otto up in that farmhouse in One Black Tooth County was what I imagined, at the time, it must have felt like to give birth. My nerves were so jangled, I could barely see. It didn't help that the week before, I'd started taking antidepressants, so I was all fuzzy-headed from my body's adjustment to the drugs. I don't remember my initial meeting with Otto as love at first sight. The family who'd been keeping him took me into the kitchen and there was a baby French bulldog in a playpen that was utterly adorable—and then Otto came in. He was jumping up on everyone, sweet as could be.

Otto had a funny little bent tail, and his eyes went in two totally different directions—a complete East-Wester—and he had some lumps on his back (I was told they were fatty tissue). But he was undeniably the cutest dog I'd ever seen. When we took him into the car I noticed his feet were all bloody. His nails had been clipped too close to the quick. I picked him up to bring him back in to get something for the bleeding and he didn't want to go in the house. He had already bonded with me, and he also really loved riding in a car. One time months later when I was walking him in Manhattan with my usual very long lead and not paying attention, I looked down and he was gone. I followed his leash into the backseat of a car; there was Otto sitting on a clean, white pillow, face forward, ready to ride. Some foolish person had left their car door open while loading it.

On the way to the home we'd be sharing, he lay on my lap, and though I acted cool, I couldn't imagine I would be able to manage life as a dog owner. When we got to the city, I walked him up my street. He didn't have any leash skills, and nor did I, but in my apartment he went straight for his bed and sat in it like he'd been there all his life. And as with everything else he did, I took it as a sign of genius.

So THERE WE WERE. That first night I felt embarrassed as I ate my dinner. I was used to living alone, and thus eating while reading the *Times*, without anyone watching. Otto's dinner was in his bowl in the kitchen, but he wasn't ready to eat and he just sat and stared at me. I felt it was rude to ignore him, or read, so I just scarfed down my meal not looking up and we moved on.

I took the week off from work and stayed with him to help

him get adjusted. There was a difficult adjustment period, mostly revolving around my chronic neurosis about leaving him alone for any more than a few minutes. I'd walk out of the apartment and tell him to stay, then I'd stand in the hallway for an hour. He never made a peep. I'd come back in from my fake shopping trip and he'd be positioned right where I told him to stay, and I'd say, "Oh no, you don't have to remain in that one spot. Just the apartment." He was good. And he was bad. He'd started snapping at people so I had to keep him on a really tight leash. Yet interestingly, there was a developmentally disabled woman who waited for her bus when I walked him in the mornings and she would run to pet him every day. She was not gentle or cautious or quiet, but Otto just knew. He never snapped at her. He let her do whatever she wanted and waited patiently till she was done, which we'd know when she'd say, "Now that's what I call a good dog!" and repeat, "Now that's what I call a good dog!"

I THOUGHT ABOUT HIM every minute we were apart, brought him everywhere the law allowed, fed him everything I ate, carried him up to my sleeping loft every night, and tucked him under the covers, his head on the pillow next to mine. All my energy was put toward making him happy. It was the best relationship I'd ever been in.

The more time we spent alone, the more I thought he was just like me. We were both on our own, we both needed someone, and we both hated being left alone. I started to realize after a week or so that I loved him.

"You're in love with him," my therapist said to me. It had been her idea for me to get a dog. She'd recently gotten two bichons frises and was overwhelmed by the number of men who approached her to chat on her walks.

Yuck, I thought, not so much for the bestiality connotations but for the idea that my new boyfriend was four-legged, flat-faced, and neutered. Somehow it made me feel like that was going to be it for me. I'd never be a part of a human couple.

As I walked him around the Upper West Side, I noticed more families and I continued to worry that people would now begin to see me as a "dog person." You know, the kind who likes dogs better than people. Or the kind who can only attract a companion who relies on her for food. I wondered if by adopting Otto, I had sealed my fate as a single woman with a dog. I could see our future together. Me and him. Otto and Julie. "Happy Holidays from Julie and Otto" accompanied by a picture of Otto dressed in a Santa hat. Well, so be it. At least I wouldn't be totally alone.

But something close to miraculous did happen. I suddenly discovered I had developed dog-vision. Prior to this point, I had not known there was a dog run two blocks from my apartment at the Museum of Natural History. *I'd never seen it though I'd walked by it thousands of times.* It was like entering the Twilight Zone or suddenly being able to see dead people but instead it was dogs and people with dogs. I'd apparently walked by these formerly invisible neighbors again and again, but only now, with Otto as my ambassador, did I stop to say hello. I had to wonder what else I had been missing. Were handsome single men all over the place, too? Thrillingly, I also got to talk to celebrities with dogs, now that we had a common denominator. While walking Otto, I met Kevin Bacon and Kyra Sedgwick, who were walking their dog. Otto peed on the ground and did his usual male-dog kicking of dirt to cover his potent scent.

Kevin gasped and said, "Wow! Did you see that? That dirt went like thirty feet!"

I said, "Yes, he's quite talented."

Kyra said, "Isn't that the kind of dog Travis wants?"

"No," Kevin said dismissively, "that's a pug."

"Oh yes," I said, determined to stay in the conversation. "Pugs."

We met Dianne Wiest and her terrier; hunky Chris Cuomo, son of the then governor Mario Cuomo, with his black Lab; Billy Baldwin and Chynna Phillips and their dog Thurman (after New York Yankee Thurman Munson); Carol Kane and her pug George. Other celebrities like Cameron Diaz and Rosie O'Donnell just stopped to pet him because he was so cute. Having Otto opened my world. I found that a good percentage of people liked to pet cute dogs, and even when they ignored me I'd get to say the never tiresome, "Say, *Thank you for petting me. I'm Otto and I love to get my tummy scratched.*" I made friends with other people though none of us knew each other's name—we were Otto's owner, Mercedes' owner, Amy's owner, and Scungilli's owner. I also couldn't count the number of times an elderly person told me that a Boston terrier had been the first dog they'd had or it was the kind of dog their aunt or uncle or grandparent had. And their names were almost always Buster. I surmised it was because they look like Buster Brown's dog, Tige, who was actually an American pit bull terrier.

I also made friends with my upstairs neighbor John, a guy who lived across the hall from his partner. He had four dogs, so he walked them a lot. We started going out on our walks together, and I liked that I didn't have to go it alone, plus we gossiped and made fun of everyone so it was good times all around. Little by little Otto implanted himself in every part of my life. I took him to parties and to bars, he slept in my bed (under the covers), and we traveled together. A month or so after I got him I took him to Barbara's office so her friend, the one who referred me, could meet him. I told him about our intense relationship and he shook his head.

"I used to be like that with Buster but not anymore," he said self-righteously. "He has his life and I have mine."

I felt like he had just called me a loser. I was the grown-up equivalent of the kid in my second-grade class who brought his stuffed bear to school every day. How the hell was Otto going to have his own life? Was he supposed to call other dogs for movie dates? And what about me? What was I going to do?

In late September, I sat with Otto on our couch and we began the process of finding him a Halloween costume. I knew he had no idea what was going on, but my enthusiasm was enough to make him know he was going to hate it. Halloween has been my favorite holiday, but after the year I went to a grown-up party dressed as the Wicked Queen from *Sleeping Beauty* and everyone else was dressed as people who are too cool for Halloween, I stopped celebrating. When I found out that there was a doggie Halloween parade at the dog run, I nearly blew a nerd gasket. Dog Halloween costumes had become increasingly popular and nowhere was that more evident than the Upper West Side dog world. I went through the costumes in the catalog, dismissing any that seemed undignified (the hot dog) or too cutesy (bunny or bumblebee) or ones that simply made no sense (Superman?). In the end, Otto and I went with a handsome Howard Hughes costume with a faux-leather aviator hat, white silk scarf, and goggles that wouldn't stay on and just swung around his neck.

On Halloween, I dressed him up and walked him to the dog run. We passed through a group of high school kids who laughed at him (or at me). One of them said to me, "Why don't you just have a kid?" Once we got to the dog run, we were insulated from that kind of attitude. Otto started chasing after a Jack Russell dressed up as Jane Russell and enjoyed a treat bag of Liv-A-Snaps and Beggin' Strips.

Every occasion was a chance to be together. I worried about doing anything that would keep me away from him too long. I cut out of work early and took the subway instead of walking home from the office to save time. I didn't want him to be lonely for one extra second. Our bond was entirely different from what I had with our family dogs growing up. Dogs who need to be walked and not just let out in the yard are much more connected to you. You know, though you may wish you didn't, their whole potty schedule, for example. My dogs growing up lay on their dog beds in the kitchen regardless of where we were, but Otto was never out of my vision.

I used to fantasize about coming home and finding a note from him: "Went to *La Bohème* and for a quick bite with Maud and Addie. Don't wait up!"

In my first years with him, we'd often go out to dinner to restaurants that had dining alfresco. Otto would start on the ground next to me and before anyone knew it, he'd be on the chair facing me. Many a passerby did a double take. Not because he was a dog at the table, but because he appeared to be a person. He was very well behaved, ignoring the bark of intractable four-legged pedestrians (it really seemed to piss them off to see him sitting at the table, those dogs who were just dogs). To me, it wasn't so much my doing as Otto's, since he insisted upon being a member of the family. The sooner everyone got that through their heads, the better.

As we got to know each other, I learned so much more about Otto:

- He didn't lick. If he was particularly excited to see you he would "snoofle" at you. That is, blow air and "wet" through his nose at you. It sounds gross when you say it, but it was really very cute. It was like a very cheery blowhole.
- If you were petting him and you stopped, he'd tap you with his paw till you started again. If you didn't start

petting him again the taps became more insistent until they were hits.

- He was an amazing soccer player. He could juggle a ball on his nose for minutes, block any shot, and dribble around multi-table legs.
- He enjoyed salmon in all ways: grilled, raw, smoked, or croquetted.
- He liked to sleep under the covers and would sometimes stand under them and bark.
- He would wear a winter coat, but refused a hooded raincoat and boots.
- He hated water for anything but drinking. If you swam he'd yell at you, and if you gave him a bath he acted like he was being violated in the worst of ways; if you took him out in the rain, he'd do an about-face.
- A veterinary ophthalmologist once told me his eyes were "exceptionally bulgy."
- He smelled like Fritos.

More than just emotionally changed by our bond, I had practically restructured my life for Otto, without even realizing it. I didn't order spicy foods because he couldn't eat them, and I always ordered enough for two. If he got up during the night, I jumped up and took him out. If he had an accident on the floor, I gave him Pepto-Bismol. I never resented anything I had to do for him. The only way I could justify leaving him for a workout was if it was before he woke up in the morning. So I'd slip out at 4:45 and return by 6:30, a full fifteen minutes before he woke up. For my whole life up to that point I had worried that I was too selfish to get married. I couldn't imagine finding someone whom I'd want to live with all the time. What if we didn't like the same TV shows? What if he didn't want to have Mexican or pizza when I wanted Mexican or pizza? What if he expected me to have six-pack abs? My fears were always about what would be taken from me, never what I might gain. It took time, but my relationship with Otto made me realize that if you love someone, you're more than willing to compromise to meet their needs—whether it be more nights of roast chicken than you would ordinarily choose, skipping an evening on the town, or not watching a television show with a barking dog.

It made me feel good to see him content. I took care of him and he took care of me. Within six months of adopting him, I grew up.

HAVING OTTO TAUGHT ME about the give-and-take that is needed to succeed in a relationship. He gave me the courage to try things and the feeling that there was someone waiting for me. If I could've turned Otto into a man, Pinocchio-style, maybe with a tad less gas and eyes that looked straight ahead, I thought at the time, I might actually be able to have a viable relationship. So what if I met a man who wanted to do nothing but watch baseball game after baseball game or eat in restaurants that scored poorly on the Department of Health's inspection? I now knew I could compromise. It might work. It was certainly worth finding out.

LESSON TWO

How to Find the Parachute Color That's Most Flattering to You

A couple of years into my life with Otto, I decided I wanted a job that would allow me to spend more time with him. I thought about writing a children's book about him called *Otto in the City*, but it probably wouldn't earn me enough to support the two of us. I needed to find a dog-inclusive career. I think somehow I also knew that were the day to come when I'd have human children, this kind of career would be useful in making time for them as well. I looked into a variety of careers that I was either unqualified for or uninterested in—like groomer, veterinary technician, receptionist for a vet office. And then my Omega Institute catalog arrived. I'd been to Omega with my mother a couple of times for various new age workshops. Located in bucolic Rhinebeck, New York, the Omega Institute for Holistic Studies is a new age retreat with classes in everything from Past Life Therapy Training to Kabbalistic Healing to Meditations and Yoga to Spring Ecstatic Chant and The Elixir of Passion to knitting with *Indiana Jones*'s own Karen Allen.

Looking through the catalog, I quickly passed over career training in topics like Feng Shui Landscaping and Bodywork Artistry. Then I fell upon the answer: I would be an animal communicator. I'd had a session with one when I first got Otto—over the phone—and she was not unlike the psychics I'd consulted for myself. She told me what Otto thought about various things in my apartment (didn't like the loft, liked the oversized mirror) and that he wanted to visit the big white house (there was a photo of my house in Katonah on the wall; I asked the animal communicator to tell Otto it had been sold). He felt my choices in dog coats were not working for him, particularly the belted ones (it sounded like a long-winded way of saying "too gay"). And he spent a good deal of time talking about food ("Save your money on the dog food, I like people food better"). All in all, I was impressed and jealous. I wanted to talk to Otto, too. Now I could learn to talk to him and every other animal on the planet. I would be Dr. Do-little-or-nothing. And I'd charge the one hundred and fifty dollars for a forty-five-minute hour that I'd shelled out. It was shaping up into a brilliant plan.

I signed up for the three-day workshop. Omega was like being at a Grateful Dead sleepaway camp, with lots of rainbow batik, white-people dreadlocks, and that vegan/vegetarian/macrobiotic food that some people who don't happen to be me really like. A few years later, I would come with my friend Barbara for a writing workshop taught by Lynda Barry and every night when we turned the lights out in our cabin, a cloud of bats swarmed in through the cracks in the eaves. I stayed under the covers emitting bursts of bloodcurdling screams while Barbara attempted to reason with them (and laughed at me). When we'd tell people at breakfast about the horrors of our night, they'd say, "Oooh, you're so lucky!" "That's a wonderful blessing!" "Oh, I wish bats came into my room!"

I took the bus upstate on Friday afternoon. It was an Omega bus but it picked you up on a street beside Penn Station. There was no need to check the sign in the bus window; Omega students were unmistakable, with their bongos, nose rings, tie-dye, and Guatemalan beads. I got on behind a woman who asked the bus driver if it was okay to bring *chapati* on the bus.

"No, no pets on the bus!" he said.

"It's bread," she clarified.

"Oh, bread's okay," he confirmed.

WE ARRIVED LATE IN the day but there was so much to do in this course over just one weekend that a Friday evening class was scheduled for 7 to 10 P.M. Our teacher was Penelope Smith, the foremost animal communicator (this was before animal communicators had their own TV shows and channels). With her oversized Coke-bottle glasses and cherubic face, she greeted the class—over one hundred students—with the kind of grin that made you think she knew a wonderful secret, which of course she did if she knew how to talk to animals. I felt very encouraged by that as I found a seat on the floor of the enormous, screened-in gazebo in the woods of Omega. We all looked at her smiling eyes and everyone got very, very quiet. There was a long pause as she looked around at the expectant faces framed by the purple dusk.

"Listen," she said and then said nothing. I guessed she didn't mean "listen to me" because she wasn't saying anything. Many students smiled knowingly and nodded as if they knew what we were listening to.

"Do you hear the crickets?" I thought it was a good sign that I had heard the crickets. How sharp my skills were already!

"What are they saying?"

I knew what they were saying: "chirp, chirp!" I was communicating with the animals. Five cents, please! There were lots of nodding heads, including mine.

Many hands went up so I raised mine, too. I was going to say, "Chirp, chirp," or maybe "Chip, chip."

She called on a woman with a deep tan on her very plump face and wild blond curls pulled back in a hand-dyed iridescent lilac bandanna. "I hear one saying"—here she paused, straining to make sure she got the message right—"it's going to rain." Penelope nodded yes; she'd apparently heard the same cricket. I slowly pulled my hand down.

Another woman whipped up her arm, very encouraged, and said, "There seems to be a lot of concern about the weather!" Interesting. The crickets were just like my grandparents' friends in Fort Lauderdale.

Now the class was on fire. The crickets were warning one another about a storm coming from the Northeast, assigning tasks of who was to bring what to the shelter ("Don't everyone bring dessert!"). There was also a pregnant cricket and another one who was mad about missing the season finale of *Home Improvement*. I walked back to my cabin alone, where I heard a squirrel say, "Hey, do you believe these people paid five hundred bucks to try to figure out what crickets are saying?"

The next morning after a breakfast of tofu-eggs and what

seemed like a seventy-five-pound whole wheat roll with ghee, I headed to the classroom, wondering who we would be talking to today—a fly? A hydra? I was very happy to see actual dogs there; I thought I had a much better chance of hearing them.

Penelope told us stories of the different animals she'd communicated with in her work and at home—she lived on a nature preserve in Point Reyes, California, a place that sounded like magickal-unicorn-rainbows-of-love land.

We were instructed to start by just listening and imagining what we heard. We each took turns with the dogs. I was beside a boxer so I decided to chat with him. I did what I was told—closed my eyes, tried to empty my mind and hear what he said. Nothing was coming and I imagined him saying, "What? What am I supposed to say?" I thought if I were him, I would not have liked having my ears and tail docked so I made him say, "I didn't like having my ears and tail docked." Later, we went around the room and I raised my hand and told Penelope what I'd "heard." She nodded that yes, he had said that. I asked her how you know if they're saying it or if you're making it up. She looked me in the eye and said, "You don't have to worry, *you're* already doing it." Me, no one else—she knew I had the gift. I looked around at all the other students with great smugness and started figuring out how I could get the money together to take Animal Communication II at the Point Reyes Commune.

What Penelope described to us about being an animal communicator was something like being in a country where you don't speak the language and then going off and learning it and coming back. It was like a switch went on and all of the voices were clear. She told us about a time when there was a great fire on her nature preserve (everything she said sounded like a plot point in a Disney movie) and she'd been so upset that for a brief period of time she couldn't hear the animals speak! She'd lost her sense. "I knew what it was like to be a 'normal' person," she said in a chilling tone.

I walked around Omega imagining every sparrow and kitty cat was talking to me. Curiously, they all seemed to have my personality.

The one thing that did ring true to me was when Penelope talked about the ways in which you were already communicating with your dog. Aside from the sit/stay/leave it type commands, you knew if your dog had to go out for a walk or they'd stand by their food bowl to tell you they were hungry. There were other things. My aunt Mattie always knew when her dog was getting a stomachache because he'd do a certain kind of stretching, and I knew when Otto needed his anal glands expressed because he'd perform a very special dance. He'd sit on the rug and with one leg drag himself around and around in circles and he'd look at me every time he came around, like a ballerina spotting during a series of pirouettes.

On the bus back to New York, I talked to people who'd taken other workshops and we all had the same self-satisfied sense that we were now in possession of superhuman abilities. We could have driven the bus back with our minds or, better yet, transported ourselves by breaking down our molecular structures. One woman who'd done some kind of automatic writing class asked me if I could talk to her cat for her (you don't need to try to convince these people—they drank the Kool-Aid in the Omega dining hall). The cat was back in San Luis Obispo, California. She showed me his picture in her wallet and asked me to see if he was okay. I stopped and concentrated hard on his picture and San Luis Obispo and I thought about the swallows in Capistrano and finally decided yes, he was okay. I had a very strong feeling that he *was*. You know, because he looked fine in the picture. Why wouldn't he be? She was really relieved because she'd talked to a friend on the phone the night before and there'd been *a hurricane* and she was worried that her cat had been scared or worse.

"He's alone?" I asked.

She gasped, "You knew that!"

No! I just couldn't believe someone would go from California to New York for four days and leave their cat alone. I worked a six-hour day and had a dog walker come in the middle of it to look in on my boy. The woman from the bus and I exchanged addresses, and she wrote to me when she got home that her house was nearly destroyed. A tree had fallen on it. But, as I'd said, the cat was fine. He'd found a safe place under the porch to hide. She was eternally grateful for my message. Maybe I had gotten a line on the cat, but more likely I'd guessed right. Much of animal communication and psychic abilities has to do with confidence, and I had none. I also knew how anxious I was to believe when someone predicted something (especially if it was positive) for me. But it kind of scared me, too. Like the stories I'd heard about people getting possessed while playing with the Parker Brothers Ouija board. I wasn't psychic. I mean, I did have those moments where I'd be singing Steely Dan's "Peg" and turn the radio on just as it was playing or pick up the phone to call my mother and she'd already be on the line because she'd just called me, or when I intuited that I wasn't going to get a job and then didn't. But what was psychic and what was coincidence? I was sure I didn't know.

I got home and picked Otto up from Barbara, who'd been watching him while I was away. I'd been trying to talk to him from Omega and asked her if he sounded like he'd been listening to me.

"Oh, yeah," she said. "Did you tell him to fart a lot?"

Barbara hadn't grown up with dogs, but she really loved them, especially Otto. This was the first time she'd ever dog-sat and she kept telling me beforehand that she was really going to freak out if she had to pick up his poop on the street. It was unbearably disgusting to her. I understood. Anyone else's dog's doo-doo grossed me out, but not Otto's. When I got back I asked her how it had gone. She said he didn't "go" the whole weekend. He peed a lot but it was like he knew she didn't want to pick it up so he didn't make one. I thought maybe Barbara was psychic, or Otto was. Back in my studio, I worked on the techniques I'd learned over the weekend, sitting quietly and listening for a word or phrase, maybe an "I love you, Julie." I didn't hear anything, but I did smell something—something very, very bad. And then I "heard" him say he needed to go out, that the doodying he hadn't been doing all weekend had caught up to him. I took him out and he "spoke" for a long, long time.

I tried very hard to practice and practice. I read Penelope's books and sat for extensive periods of time with Otto. He was usually sleeping and when he wasn't I tried to talk to him. I'd close my eyes and then I'd fall asleep. My brother Matt said he believed all dogs thought the same thing and Otto was no different: "A string of hot dogs, a piece of bacon, a chicken leg, cheese, pizza, a ham sandwich . . ." When I first started dating my future husband I would tell him over and over again how smart Otto was, mostly because of the depth of his expressions. "Maybe," Paul said. "And maybe he's really, really dumb."

"Maybe you are!" I came back.

On a blowy, gray autumn day, Otto and I were walking down Columbus Avenue when I saw a familiar face. It was one of the assistants from the Animal Communication workshop. Finally, I'd get a glimpse into Otto's thoughts and see if I had in fact been reading him correctly. Sweet affirmation! I was excited to introduce her to my amazing canine. She stooped, gently cupping Otto's face in her hands, and began staring deeply into his walleyes. And . . . he bit her. It was later communicated to me that I needed to pay her medical bills.

As for me, I stopped trying to do ESP with him and started talking out loud to him. On Thursdays, I had therapy at 4:30 followed by group therapy at six. It was just too long a day to leave him in my apartment so I took him to doggie day care. The first place, Canine Country, was a few blocks from my apartment and it was like a ballroom for dogs. I chose it because it was $15 a day instead of the $20 some of the other more high-end places charged. It seemed good. Dogs running all around going to the bathroom on the floor and then a guy in scrubs would come clean it up. I left Otto with a lot of hugs and kisses and promises that I'd be back later. It was gnawing at me the whole day, and I ran to pick him up at 7:30 on the dot. When I walked into the place there were big dogs running all around barking and playing, and in the corner I saw Otto sitting alone with his ears down, looking just like a baby seal. He wasn't playing with anyone. He probably thought I wasn't coming back. He saw me and we had a *Love Story*–worthy reunion. The guy in scrubs assured me that Otto had had a great time, that he was just worn-out now. When we got outside, Otto took a pee that lasted several minutes and I realized he was such a good dog, so totally housebroken, that he wouldn't *go* on their stupid floor. And they didn't take them outside for walks (which was why it was cheaper). I was infused with guilt, and I wasn't about to leave him there again. Plus, he stunk like a mall pet store.

The following week I did some research and found a better option, the tonier Yuppie Puppie that was located on the ground floor of a brownstone and had a backyard and a kiddie pool with a slide—plus those dogs did get walked. I felt infinitely better leaving him there and when I picked him up he wasn't exploding with pee. I now had a solid plan, and I felt very satisfied. The next week Otto started pulling back as soon as we got on the block where the Yuppie Puppie was located. I dragged him to the top of the stairs leading down to the entrance.

"This is the good place, Otto, you liked it!" I pleaded. "It's not that place with the big smelly floor." People passed me by giving me a "My dog is more obedient than yours" expression.

"Otto, I am going to be gone for eleven hours! You can't

stay home alone!" I tried again to take him down the stairs, but he would not budge. Anyone with a dog knows about this suction-cup feature that enables a twenty-five-pound dog to render himself immobile. You suddenly find yourself attempting to walk the Great Pyramid of Giza.

"Listen, I have to go to work, and if you're not willing to go down these stairs you are going to have to go home, where you will be alone all day." He stared at me with his lips tightly closed. "It's your choice, buddy. You can stay here and have fun and frolic or be by yourself in the apartment with no one to talk to or play with or run with, no sing-alongs, no pool." He started gingerly prancing in the direction of home.

"Okay," I said, "it's your choice. You chose this. I was willing to pay the twenty bucks, plus this week I was going to pay extra for real bacon treats! Okay. Your decision. Your bed, you can lie in it." We got back to the door of my apartment and I started arguing again. "Otto, you can't stay alone in the apartment all day!"

Pause. "Really."

Pause. "Think about it, huh?"

I looked around as he tried to go up the stairs. I couldn't leave him there for so long. And before you wonder, yes, I knew it was totally about me and my neuroses. Clearly he'd held his bladder that long at Canine Country, but I knew I'd be too miserable leaving him in the nice cool apartment with the classical radio and plates of food. So I walked him over to my aunt Mattie's. Otto had fixed it so that instead of being stuck at the Yuppie Puppie he went to Mattie's Doggy Heaven every Thursday. I'd drop him off before work and pick him up with his newly fattened belly after group. Though it was a half-hour cab ride, it came out monetarily very close to a day in doggie day care.

He had finally, unmistakably, communicated with me. And I understood. But it felt more like common sense than actual animal communication. I knew there was no way I was going to continue in this field; it just wasn't me. I believed there were people who communicated with animals, like Penelope Smith, but I wasn't one of them.

There is great value in putting your toe in the water. A good friend of mine always wanted to be a doctor. In her senior year of high school she took a job in a hospital. The smell there made her sick. She threw up every day. It was pretty clear that being a doctor would have to come off the table, but what a fantastic revelation. We all need to find what's comfortable for us, and sometimes the only way to do it is to find out what doesn't fit. I was glad I'd taken animal communication, but what became clear to me from the experience was that my favorite part of it was telling the stories. And being with my dog. And it turns out writers *can* bring their dogs to work.

LESSON THREE

How to Keep the Yin from Strangling the Yang

When I was four months pregnant with my daughter, Otto died. It was unexpected and devastating. He wasn't ill that anyone knew of, and he wasn't that old. I had planned for him to be a big part of the birth. In my mental rehearsal, I would feel contractions, call Mattie, she'd pick us all up, drop Paul and me off at the hospital, and take Otto back to her apartment so she could dog-sit. When I realized he was gone, I was despondent, breathless, and broken. There was such an immense black hole within me that I worried it would hurt my unborn child. I sat staring into space for long periods of time trying to connect to Otto and find out if he was planning on being reincarnated. I just wanted to get him again. Looking at photos of new puppies online, I calculated the date of their birth to see if it could be him, like his soul might have slipped out of Otto and into Henry. I was trying to get a sign: *"Are you him?"* In the meantime, people were gently suggesting that it wasn't a good time for a new puppy. Well, not so gently, more like screaming, *"Are you nuts? You're going to get a puppy right before you have a new baby?"* My brother Brian would call, then his wife, Cheryl, then my parents. If you know me even a little, you would realize that telling me (and Paul) not to do something because you know better ain't gonna work. We ignored them.

When we ended up getting a new Boston terrier puppy, there was no doubt in my mind. This wasn't Otto. Otto was like Yoda, but the new pup was a fresh spirit, unencumbered by depth—kind of vapid. She was born to my former vet's dog in a duplex brownstone on Central Park West. She was hardly a rescue, unless you feel strongly about having a doorman. Beatrice was just herself. And with that new baby on the way, a part of me was relieved that she didn't have Otto's breadth of requirements. I decided that the new dog would be just a dog. I lay on the couch on my side and Beatrice lay on my expansive belly. She was under ten pounds, a feather. If Otto had done that, the baby would've been crushed. A few months later, I had my daughter and the baby/puppy combo *was* challenging. I would be in the apartment, Bea would be jumping up and down because she had to go out, and there would be Violet sleeping away in her bassinet. You would have thought the act of taking the baby out in her stroller while holding Bea's leash was like landing a jet on an aircraft carrier in the middle of the ocean at midnight. I was so uncoordinated that if, God forbid, my cell phone rang, I would freeze. Before too long, though, I was able to juggle them all and text a grocery list at the same time.

It didn't take me long to realize my new baby was not like a dog at all, even apart from the physical differences. I was actually quite pleased that when she had to go to the bathroom, I didn't have to take her outside. It was easy! Well, maybe not *so* easy. We were living in a one-bedroom at the time, so Bea slept with us and Violet slept right beside us in her bassinet. One night after we'd all gone to sleep we were awoken by a bloodcurdling scream from Violet. We jumped up, turned on the lights, and looked in her crib, expecting to see a snake coiled around her. Nothing. It was nothing. She didn't even wake up from it. (Damn kids!) We went back to sleep and about an hour later, I was still only half dozing and my leg hit something wet in the bed. I turned the light on and apparently Bea's dinner didn't agree with her—she'd thrown up all over the sheets. I woke Paul so I could get everything off and we both fell asleep on the bare mattress for a cool hour and a half. These were not the best of times. When people asked about a second child we both looked at them like they were stark raving lunatics.

There isn't a hard-and-fast rule about when you're supposed to spay your female dog—some say to try to do it before the first menstruation. That's what we were hoping for. It was a bad year for timing, and when I saw the spots of blood all over the house I briefly considered throwing myself out the window. ("Why not Bea?" Paul asked. "You weren't the one bleeding.") The one thing we knew was Bea couldn't sleep in our bed at this time. It was just too gross even for us. So after about fifty phone calls and e-mails throughout the day between Paul and me, we decided she'd sleep in her crate that night. The crate we got when she was born, the one she'd been inside exactly once—to take the biscuit and leave. That night we put her in it with her little plush panda and some beef sticks (her favorite), dusted our hands off, and patted ourselves on the back.

First, she scratched at the front of the crate. Once, twice, eight-hundred-million times. Then she started crying (while still scratching). Crying and scratching. Scratching and crying. Her crate was in our bedroom and slowly it started to hop-hop-hop across the floor. Keep in mind, she was under ten pounds. So Paul, the toughie, picked up her box, put it out in the living room, closed the bedroom door, and we went to sleep . . . in theory. Her cries became more insistent and then changed into a sound I've never heard from a dog—it was more like the bleating of a sheep or the crying of a baby (well, a baby with a Mayor of Munchkinland kind of voice). I popped up in bed and stared at Paul, who was fast asleep and snoring. Any new mother is familiar with this scenario, but the baby was asleep. I poked Paul. "Listen to Bea!"

He opened his eyes, wrinkled his face at the sound, and then started dozing again.

"What are we going to do?" I said.

"Just don't listen," he answered.

"I can't not listen, she's going to hurt herself."

"What do you want me to do?"

"Go check on her."

Paul dutifully went out and Bea flipped upon seeing him. He told her to be quiet and go to sleep and came back to bed and he went back to sleep. I sat up listening as her already keening wails increased in intensity and volume.

"I can't stand it," I told Paul. "I'm going to go into the living room and sleep with her."

I came out and she started screaming at me. I closed our bedroom door and let her out of her crate. I opened up the pullout couch, put on spare sheets and a blanket and pillows, and picked Bea up and put her in the bed with me. After about ten seconds she jumped off the bed and started scratching at our bedroom door.

"Stop it!" I scream-whispered. "Get over here."

I walked over and put her back and she continued to escape. "What is the problem?" I asked her. "I'm here in a bed. I just came out here for you. I don't want to sleep out here either!"

She wanted to go in the bedroom—the bedroom was her room, not the living room. At this point, it was two or three in the morning and I'd not been to sleep yet. And I was sleep deprived before I even went to bed. I was starting to get deranged. She wouldn't stop scratching at the door and if she woke the baby, I would kill her. I had an idea. I'd put one of Violet's tiny newborn swaddling diapers on Bea and she could come in the bed with us. If you don't know this already, dogs and babies are not exactly the same shape. Even when babies crawl, it's a very, very different structure. So I slipped the diaper on Bea . . . and it fell off . . . and I put it on . . . and it fell off. Growing more insane, I took a roll of packing tape out, put the diaper back on her, and started madly taping. Good. I opened the door and let her in the room. Paul was out cold. Bea jumped on the bed and got under the covers, leaving her little tapey diaper on the floor behind her. I started to cry and think that maybe in the morning I'd be able to have myself committed to a mental institution—just for a couple of days, so I could sleep. I went to the hall closet and got a huge beach towel and put it in our bed and woke Paul up to say, "I'm so sorry. I'm so sorry for being very, very crazy; please don't divorce me." He said it was okay and everyone finally settled down, and as Paul snored, I wept and told him how much I loved him.

At the first possible moment, we had Beatrice "fixed." So, you know, she wouldn't leak anymore. Slowly things began to calm down. Violet turned one and it seemed like a good time to have baby number two, but not in that one-bedroom. We moved a few blocks north to an apartment that would accommodate more family members. We even gave Violet the larger bedroom so she could share it with her future brother or sister (Florence or Lawrence). Around the time we decided to start having purposeful sex, our finances went screaming south. It just wasn't a good time to add another dependent, as I lovingly referred to our future potential child. So Violet got a great big room and another year went by and our money situation kept getting worse.

We needed an escape route. So Paul, Violet, Beatrice, and I went to stay at my parents' house for the summer—we needed to regroup and not get any further in the rent-hole.

Violet was pretty much happy there once we got past the initial transition, but I wasn't. I was certain that Beatrice felt the way I felt. One day she was outside and got stung by something on her eye—she looked like Jake LaMotta. She walked up to me and I swore she said, "Can we please go home now?"

Bringing your dog to someone else's home is always a dicey issue, whether they have dogs or not. If they don't have dogs they are completely freaking out about the carpets and furniture; and if they do have dogs, they expect them all to be treated the same way. When I was growing up, my parents treated our dogs very much like, well, dogs. They weren't issued additional coats in the winter or given rain boots. They ate their dog food from their dog bowl, and they didn't beg at the table. They lay in their dog beds—not on the furniture. And this was still how they ran their dog ship.

We did not. Beatrice very nearly had a seat at the table in our home and there was no furniture or rug that was off-limits to her. My dad was very concerned about this special rug he had that was colored with vegetable dye. I'm not really sure why, but you cannot pee on it. And Bea didn't. (But Violet did.)

I think because their dogs were so much bigger than Beatrice, my parents and their dogs didn't begrudge her lying on the couch with the people at cocktail hour. I remember the first time I went to their house with Otto. They had recently put down wall-to-wall sea-foam carpeting in the upstairs. Definitely no dogs allowed. That didn't apply to Otto. "He doesn't see color," I'd tell my father. Dad wasn't amused. I watched him stand at the foot of the stairs, Otto at the top, head cocked, with my dad yelling, *"Get down here, fatty!"* Otto looked at him, considered the offer, and went back to my mother's dressing room to lie in the sun. Sea foam wasn't his choice, and it wasn't his problem either.

I am not sure their dogs were aware that Bea was even a dog. To them she was more of a doglet, and she quickly tired of being disrespected. When the summer came to an end, we all happily returned to the city with plans to get to work, make lots of money, and not have another kid, yet.

I felt the space within me that was filled with the longing for another child quickly transformed into a desire for another dog. When I brought it up to Paul, he was very emphatically against it. Primarily, he felt that we were just getting back on our feet. Why would we want to complicate things? And there was also the cost and the time. Paul wanted to wait until things settled down a bit before getting back to the business of having a second kid. I felt entirely ambivalent about the second kid. Well, not so much ambivalent as terror-stricken by the thought. Kid number one was now walking and talking and sleeping at night and using the bathroom. A new baby would be like starting at square one. It was all sort of out there in the ether of the relationship; we weren't ready for anything at the moment so it was all hypothesis. And one of the unexpected side effects of our summer away was that now Violet was afraid to sleep alone. So she slept in the bed with us. And Bea. When I went to the gynecologist, she asked me what birth control I was using. I said, "My daughter and our dog sleep in our bed." She didn't ask any further questions.

In the meantime, we both started working again. I was writing from home on a computer that insisted on taking me to the Internet to look at dogs, specifically Boston terriers in need of rescue. There was always the thought that somewhere I'd find the reincarnated Otto who I'd imagined would have his identifying feature, the walleyes. I also thought he'd be back in Pennsylvania. The largest site for this sort of search is Petfinder.com, which kept leading me to Bostons who were in the custody of Northeast Boston Terrier Rescue. I went to the website and read the description.

> Northeast Boston Terrier Rescue (NEBTR) is comprised of volunteers based in NY/NJ and PA and serves Boston Terriers in need within reach of our helping hands. Most dogs in foster care for placement are adolescent to adult dogs in need of rehoming in life for a multitude of reasons and will need caring hands to guide them as they transition into new homes. All of our rescue dogs are fostered and evaluated for a two-week minimum to allow us to assess their personality and provide them with basic foundation skills—House/Crate

> training, basic manners—to ease their transition into new homes. It is our belief such work in foster care better prepares dogs for success and helps form lasting bonds.

I clicked on a link called "Success Stories" with photos and stories of the dogs saved. One in particular stood out. It was a studio portrait photo of a Boston terrier whose tongue was hanging out of his mouth. His name was Champ and it said, "This attractive fellow is Champ. Champ was abused by his former owners. His jaw was broken and never set, so his tongue hangs out of his mouth. His new owners report this just adds to his wonderful personality! Champ now has a caring wonderful family who love him and his flaws."

I FELT A STINGING in my eyes and a lump in the pit of my stomach. I needed to help dogs like Champ. Dogs like Otto.

I read on about what the volunteers did. It sounded perfect. I could help these dogs without getting one. In fact, it would be far better for all involved to help several rather than just one. The idea of doing volunteer work appealed to me as well. I had just cut out a quote from Marion Wright Edelman: "Service is the rent we pay to be living. It is the very purpose of life and not something you do in your spare time." My grandmother drove buses of veterans during World War II, my mother and father taught disabled kids and mentored, and everyone in my family was heavily involved in various Jewish organizations. I sent an e-mail asking if I could help and got an application back.

Hello Julie.

I am the moderator for the welcome list and received your application to join the Northeast Boston Terrier Rescue group (NEBTR).

We are always delighted to have new volunteers. Could you give me a little information about yourself, please?

1) Who referred you to NEBTR, or how did you come to us? **Internet search.**
2) Since we are a rescue group, our main objective is to assist in helping the many Bostons in need. We like to have on file a member's full name and address, with phone numbers and e-mail.
3) Have you any experience with Rescue? **I adopted a rescue whom I had for ten years.**
4) Who do you live with? **Husband and three-year-old daughter, and female Boston (spayed) (age three also).**

There are many ways in which members can help. Please let us know what you could do:

Helping in transporting Bostons to and from homes: **I don't have a car.**

Pulling and transporting dogs from shelters: **Yes, in the five boroughs.**

Fostering of Bostons until a forever home is found: **Yes** [kind of bold of me since I had yet to discuss it with the husband, but two weeks? That seemed okay].

Fund-raising . . . making or donating items to raise funds: **Yes.**

If this sounds like an organization you would like to be with, then please let me know.

If you have any questions or need assistance, please feel free to contact me.

Sheryl Trent
Northeast Boston Terrier Rescue

I sent the form back and got another e-mail from Sheryl thanking me and telling me that without a car I probably wouldn't be called on to transport and with a three-year-old child, they most likely wouldn't be able to give me a dog to foster since they didn't really know what those dogs' personalities were like and wouldn't want to risk injuring my child. I would be able to do visits to prospective homes (in the New York metro area) when they came up. In the meantime I could familiarize myself with the Yahoo! group listings to get a sense of what they did.

I was slightly disappointed, because fostering sounded fun, but also excited that I had committed to do something. And in a couple of years when Violet was older, maybe then I would be able to help more.

Joining an existing Yahoo! group is like coming into a foreign language class that's already under way. They're all talking in acronyms and using terminology you've yet to learn. The first post I read said something about an HC. I Googled HC and it said: "Hors Concours," which meant non-competing. Well, when the rescue group used it, it meant Home Check—the home visit that was done for every prospective foster or adoptive home. I was going to have to get an HC before I would be able to foster, though that didn't seem to be in the cards for the near future.

There was a lot going on all the time. The postings involved issues with fosters, requests for someone to foster or for the group to get ready for a mass of incoming (from a puppy mill or just various people surrendering at the same time), information about upcoming fund-raisers, links to Boston terriers in shelters in the area, links to Bostons on Craigslist, warnings about pet food recalls, a lost-dog notice, and the occasional "OT" (off-topic), which was usually a joke or a poem. I had a feeling it was going to be one of those things where I'd join up but never really be a part of it . . . like the pregnancy Yahoo! group I'd joined and dropped.

About two weeks into it, my attention started to drift. Everything in the group seemed to be happening in York, Pennsylvania, or Rochester, New York.

And then, as so many stories begin, one night the phone rang. It took me a while to understand what was happening. The intake coordinator of the group, Jane, had gotten my number from Sheryl. It turned out there was a Boston puppy, an eight-month-old, whose owner wanted to surrender him because she worked so much that he was spending all of his time in, and she was spending all of her money on, doggie day care. She'd bought him at a pet store on a whim even though she'd never had a dog and knew nothing about Bostons. I said, "Yes, yes," and "Oh, the poor dog," and "Oh, the dumb owner." I called Paul and told him the good news and he said, "We're going to end up keeping him, right?" And I said, "Of course not! Two-week foster!" And he said, "He's going to sleep in our bed, right?" And I said, "No, he's not." I wanted to get him, assess him, and move him out so we'd be available for the next one. Sure it would be hard. I'd read the posts about the failed foster homes. Those wimpy people who fell in love with the dogs and couldn't let them go. That would never be me.

First, we had to have our home check. We were great, our home was fine, and Beatrice introduced a growling, snapping aspect into her personality that made me think we'd flunk for sure. We didn't. It turned out that her reaction was "normal" and Jill, the volunteer, recommended introducing any potential foster to Beatrice outside on neutral territory. Little did Jill know that Beatrice considered the entire borough of Manhattan to be her territory.

Now it was all approved and I just had to make arrangements with the owner, Charlotte, for the transfer. She e-mailed a bio and pictures of Hank. He was very cute and sweet. She had not yet had time to get him neutered but she would give us the money for that and he was "pretty much housebroken."

I met Charlotte in a pocket park by my home. Hank was bigger than his pictures and he was a little hyper, but you know, he was a puppy and probably very nervous about this trip. I had Bea come out for the neutral meeting; there was a good deal of snarling and barking as we took the dogs up to my apartment. Hank flew into the apartment jumping from chair to couch to dining-room table. "He's nervous," I told Paul. "Me too," said Paul. Hank finally wound down and went to his bed, where he gnawed on his rawhide. Charlotte got teary-eyed as she prepared to say good-bye. She looked at him resting in his bed and said to him, "Why couldn't you always act like this?" (Red flag! Hmm, but didn't she say she was giving him up because she worked so much?) She handed over his papers from the pet store and the vet and signed the surrender forms I'd downloaded earlier, and where it said "Donation," she said, "Well . . . he was fifteen hundred dollars!" In other words, she'd already donated to the pet store. I was anxious about the whole scene and figured the sooner she left, the sooner everyone would settle down, so I didn't push it. I did remind her that she'd said she'd pay for the neutering and she told me to let her know the cost when it was done.

And Charlotte left. And Hank did not.

It was evening so we were all settling down to bed, or we tried to while Hank flew from chair to bed to head. Violet was in a self-taught earthquake position, crouched, head tucked under, beneath the table. There was no crate for him; there was no off switch for him. Apparently, what was meant by "pretty much housebroken" was "he pisses and craps wherever the hell he feels like." All night long he barked and flew and yelped and . . . bit.

In the morning I called Sheryl from my cell phone as I walked to the gym. It was our first conversation. She had a big laugh, a smoky voice, and an Australian accent. I did a five-minute monologue on the Horrors of Hank and how wrong Charlotte's description of him was. She listened and waited till I finished.

"First thing, love," she said gently, "when owners are surrendering, many times they will say anything."

"You mean lie?" I said, and she laughed.

She gave me some suggestions to calm Hank and told me to set up his neuter appointment; she explained the protocol about the billing and I told her that Charlotte was paying.

When I got home, I e-mailed Charlotte. She answered right away asking how Hank was doing. She said she'd been extremely worried about him. I told her he was fine and she was relieved. I told her that I was arranging his neutering and she didn't respond. The next day I e-mailed again to tell her the appointment had been set up and that it was going to be about four hundred and fifty dollars, not including post-op pain medication. Again, silence. A couple of days later she sent a reply that she'd been in Hawaii and got my e-mail and that four hundred and fifty dollars was too expensive; she offered to pay half. I was livid. Here I was taking in her effing dog that she didn't give a whit about. I called Sheryl.

I spewed my unedited thoughts about Charlotte's behavior. I was shocked! Simply shocked. Sheryl was not. "Welcome to rescue," she said.

As it turns out in life, very little ends up being how you think it's going to be. You know the Yiddish proverb *"Mann traoch, Gott lauch"*: "Man plans, God laughs." My grand plan was to join a rescue group because it would be *less* of an emotional investment than getting a second dog. Kind of like thinking that having a different date every night is easier than a steady boyfriend or girlfriend. What I saw about fostering was that in addition to the obvious difficulties of taking in a surrendered dog, you also weren't keeping them forever so in a sense you had to stay on an emotional leash—or not and then end up keeping the dog.

I started to see that there was a strong learning curve, and that the rhythm of rescue involved expecting anything at any time. But being part of a group helping hundreds of dogs a year was so amazingly rewarding. I felt like I was more than a drop in the bucket; I was on a team of superheroes. Doing the work helped me to figure out that giving was a crucial part of my fabric. It was only when I began to help give voice to these creatures who cannot speak or ask for help for themselves that I felt the balance come into my own life.

LESSON FOUR

How to Listen to That Still, Small Voice

Our first foster, Hank, it seemed, had some deep issues. We read articles and books about how to deal with them and correct his behavior. This was a new frontier for me since I'd never trained any of my own dogs. In fact, when Otto came to me, he understood the commands "sit," "stay," and even "roll over." After a few months, I had unlearned him. With me it became clear to him that he got what he wanted whether he sat or stood on his head and no longer had use for commands. Every so often he'd sit when I asked him to, but his heart wasn't in it. Occasionally, he'd do it for guests, like someone who picks up a child's yo-yo at a party. ("It's something like this, right?") Once I had a dog trainer come to my home to help me teach him. I was concerned about his snapping at certain people. She walked into my apartment with a little bag of dry cat food X's that she used to reward the dogs and her eyes fell on a plastic plate on the floor on which I'd lined up several kinds of treats including deli meats.

"What's that?" she asked.

"That's his snack tray," I replied.

"I don't think I'm going to be able to get him to obey for my Friskies when he's got his own buffet."

Later when we were outside walking she told me to make him go left when he wanted to go right. I looked at her. What was on the left? If he wanted to go right, I saw no problem with this. Finally she told me that Otto didn't need a trainer; I did.

So here I was years later wishing that I had gotten one. One article by a respected dog trainer said that when the puppy bites you, you should make a noise like a hurt puppy. I gave this nugget of wisdom to Paul and watched him respond to Hank's nips with a high-pitched yowl. *"Yee!"* he yelled. Though it made me laugh really hard, it had zero effect on Hank.

We quickly passed the two-week mark. Charlotte, the owner, ceased to exist, it seemed, and never came across with a cent. At the end of each week, I sent the directors of the group an update on Hank's progress—of which there was none. The first one I creatively called "Hank's Pupdate." The next one was simply "hank." Rather than settle in, he got worse and worse. I didn't care about the chewing of shoes and dolls, or the fact that every time we turned our backs on him he'd be standing on our dining-room table, face in a plate. I could even bear the relentless barking, but when he took flight, his mouth wide open, heading our way, we all got really unnerved. We gave him a circus name: Hank the flying biting clown dog. (We pretended he was funny, so Violet wouldn't be so frightened.) Returning from the playground one day we opened our apartment door and Hank's teeth sunk into Violet's arm. She was physically hurt, but worse than that, her feelings were hurt. I told Sheryl and Jane that we weren't the right people to foster him. I suggested military school. They called a guy in the group who had taken some other bad seeds and turned them into upstanding dogs and he agreed to take a stab at Hank. We were looking at a minimum wait of a week to get a transport set up since the guy lived eight hours upstate. Mattie lent us her car so Paul could meet the guy halfway and we could get Hank out of our lives sooner. Once he was going, which he seemed to know, he was pretty much in a constant state of ballistic. We just ducked and covered, ducked and covered. It was like *Hope and Glory.*

With all that, we still felt sad when we watched him drive

away, his face plastered against the back window of the car. After all, it wasn't his fault he'd never been socialized. It's an owner's job to teach manners.

I spent a lot of time ruminating over what was behind the surrendering of a dog. In my mind, there was a list of what I considered compelling reasons to give up your dog, and other reasons that stunk. I was always most struck by people who put so much energy into getting a dog and then dumped it. My therapist, who has the two bichons frises, met someone with a bichon puppy who was going to put the dog in a shelter—and she asked to take the dog, certain she could find it a home. It was a terrific, smart, cute puppy with a normal puppy's energy. In the end my therapist's daughter took her. The bizarre part of the tale was what came with this puppy to my therapist's home:

- four expensive plush dog beds
- five baby blankets
- twelve dog bowls
- a large box of ear wipes, eye wipes, paw wipes, and butt wipes
- a case of wee-wee pads and holders
- over thirty plush toys and twenty-seven rubber toys
- six bottles of shampoo
- five brushes and combs

- a case of treats
- a huge cloth box that had been hand-painted "Toy Box"
- clothes: a white tank with a BeDazzled "S" (the puppy's name was Sophie); three pairs of flannel pajamas (top and bottoms) with baby ducks, rattles, and blocks printed on them; four hooded sweatshirts, two with sparkles, two without (for working out, I guess); a red T-shirt with embroidered and beaded hearts, a pink T-shirt that said, "Does this shirt make me look fat?", a red T-shirt that said, "Princess" (the "i" was dotted with a heart), a pink T-shirt that said, "Little Miss Tiny"; some dressier sweaters.

The outfits. *The outfits!* How on earth do you go from a person who spends hundreds of dollars at posh Manhattan pet shops on clothes and grooming items to a person who leaves a dog at a shelter? Not even looking into rehoming! The whole thing is so puzzling. I remembered getting an engraved birth announcement from a couple who'd bought a dog. Six months later I saw them and asked them about the "baby." "Oh," the wife said, "we gave her to my uncle. She chewed everything and messed all over the floor!"

A puppy that chewed on things and wasn't housebroken? Why didn't you put it on a chain gang? It was mind-boggling, but not something that infuriated me, until I was the one taking in these castoffs. We're not talking about a family who has to give up a dog because of allergies or discovering upon the birth of a child that the dog is aggressive, or someone who has to move to an elder care facility. I'm just thinking of people who put more effort into researching the aspects of owning a car than what it takes to have a dog.

AFTER THAT Paul and I agreed that our family was not up to the job of fostering dogs. We couldn't take that kind of risk. There were still many ways I could help the rescue organization, and before long I was assigned my first home check, then my second, then my third, and on.

Pretty much everyone who wanted to adopt a Boston terrier in Manhattan lived in a fifth-floor walk-up, or so it seemed to me. I would arrive at these apartments breathless and say, "You do know"—huffing and puffing—"that Boston terriers' legs"—gag—"are very, very short"—catching breath—"don't you?" I didn't discount them for that, unless they were looking to adopt a senior dog, in which case I still didn't want to reject them. It's a very unique position, sizing up someone to possibly adopt one of our guys. As I'd ride the subway to 135th Street or St. Marks Place, I'd think about the process adoptive parents go through before being allowed to adopt a child, while the people who got pregnant themselves were under no such scrutiny. In the case of our Bostons, we were the guardians and they were our charges. We couldn't be responsible for backyard breeders or pet shop sellers not investigating the homes, but we could do it and at least we knew we were placing our rescues in homes where we'd be comfortable placing our own dogs.

Most people tried very hard. You could see they'd cleaned up and they listened carefully to questions. One woman opened the door, never looking at me, and led me to the living room, where she kept her eyes glued to the Animal Planet channel. It wasn't an act to show me she was an animal lover. She was just very weird. But a lot of excellent pet owners were not necessarily people I wanted to hang out with. I sort of liked to think of myself as a moderate, between the crazy animal people and the people who saw pets as disposable. The home checks I did in the city were vastly different from the ones in rural areas, because New York apartments generally didn't have fenced-in yards. Many people who look to rescue a dog have had one before and know what it involves. And they're attracted to a breed for a reason. As an apartment dweller with Boston terriers, I had a lot of insight to offer, and could highly recommend them as city dogs. I felt particularly connected to the applicants who'd seen a dog on our website and were applying for them. Many times a photo that gets to someone triggers something. It's like the way I want to take every dog whose eyes are bulgy and go in different directions. My cousin Mandi, who is a veterinary technician and has worked in many shelters, cautions against picking a dog who looks like a dog who has died, because of course it's not that dog and she feels like the owners can become disappointed when they see that. Her mother had a beloved English bulldog who passed away and was followed by another one who looked like the first one but was not. She actually hated the new one, and true to her prediction, it outlived her. But having taken Beatrice on the heels of Otto and knowing they were nothing alike and still being okay about it, I wasn't so sure. I definitely agreed with keeping expectations realistic. I also knew people who would get the same breed of dog over and over and keep naming them the same thing (Sparky 1, Sparky 2, Sparky 3) and it didn't seem to bother them (though I can't speak for the Sparkys).

I'd been busy with work and not paying as much attention to the list as normal when I got a call on my cell phone while I was at the gym. It was about ninety-five degrees outside and I had to dry off repeatedly to hear the message. It was Sheryl and she said it was urgent.

I called her back and she boiled down the story. There was

a woman with a found Boston in the West Village who was going to dump the dog in the city pound if someone didn't get him TO-DAY. Violet was with a babysitter so I used the opportunity to get the dog (someone in Pennsylvania was set to foster but she couldn't pick up the dog immediately). Sheryl said I should call Joy, the volunteer in Pennsylvania, because she'd been in touch with the woman. I called her as I started to walk. I didn't know Joy, but after two minutes I felt like I'd known and loved her my whole life. She's from the Deep South and she works as a psychiatric nurse.

"Okay, you ready, Julie?" she asked, took a deep breath, and said, "So last week Sheryl gets a call from this woman saying a guy in her office found this nice Boston in New Jersey and he was going to keep him, but his mother wouldn't let him. Now I don't know why this guy lives with his mother but, anyway, he took the dog into the city and gave her to the woman. I talked to her myself and told her I'd meet her anywhere, but not in New York City because I'm afraid to drive there. So she told me she'd be going out to the Hamptons for the weekend and she'd bring the dog halfway and meet up with Cindy [another volunteer], and then right before this was supposed to take place, she canceled because she didn't have a ride. So I talked to Sheryl and she said tell her to take a car service and *we will pay* for it, but she wouldn't, so then I get a call from her today saying, 'You have to take him now or I'm bringing him to the pound.' So that's where you come in."

I took everyone's phone numbers and called the woman, whose name was Coco, and asked her if she could bring the dog to me. She told me she didn't have money for that (but she did have money to take the dog to the pound, which was farther?). I asked for her address and told her I could jump on the subway and be right there. She said I should just meet her at the West Fourth Street basketball courts, which I knew from my NYU days.

I arrived within twenty minutes and waited for her to come. I watched for her to show up from all directions and saw a very thin young woman wearing a black slip, black stiletto heels, and Victoria Beckham–type sunglasses. She seemed nice, definitely on drugs, but at least she was a dog lover.

Immediately she apologized for not being able to bring the dog, whom she'd named Mr. Man, up to my area. I said it was fine. She said she'd brought the dog to a vet in her neighborhood who'd scanned and found a microchip and gave her the number of "some ranch" but she threw it away. She didn't even call, because she KNEW this dog had been abused. He was panting and acting very anxious, but it was sweltering and she was nutty so I couldn't really assess the situation. Having come from the gym I didn't have any of my stuff with me—a leash, harness, or crate. She had some sort of wiry rope device attached to a scarf around his neck that she said I could keep. He wasn't interested in her good-bye; in fact, when I took the rope from her, he just started running and running and every ten feet he would stop and have explosive diarrhea. I had one bag with me, and he must have gone forty times. Now I was going to have to figure out how to get him the hundred blocks back to my apartment. I called information for a pet taxi service but they had no one available to help me so I bought some water and sat in the shade for a minute. Mr. Man jumped at something and I cut my hand on his rope trying to subdue him. Blood started oozing down my arm and got on my shirt and legs and Mr. Man started crapping again. People looked at me like a bloody, sweaty woman in disgusting gym clothes with a crapping dog . . . which was accurate. I wanted to shout, "I'M A VERY FANCY LADY! I SHOP ONLY IN THE FINEST OUTLETS!" It was useless. I couldn't scream, *"Cut"* or even *"Help!"* Help what? Help me plug this dog's butt long enough for me to get him in an air-conditioned taxi! I called Paul, who was at work in Soho, and left him a message to call me. I waited and waited and as I was about to give up, whatever that meant, I looked straight ahead and saw Kettle of Fish, a bar owned by my husband's friends Adrian and Patrick. I dragged Mr. Man up to the door and looked in. Paul and I had stopped there many times over the years. Adrian was never, ever there. Today she was standing by the door. Dressed in gauzy white, she was my angel. She gave Mr. Man a bowl of water, which he inhaled, and she refilled it two more times. She gave me some paper towels and a Band-Aid and somehow the cool dark bar had the effect of a dose of Pepto-Bismol because the Man stopped his eruptions. I wiped him up, carried him out the door, and hailed a cab. I held him tightly to me, praying to the God of humiliation to please not let him lose control in the cab. As if by a miracle, he made it up to my street. The minute we stepped out of the cab, he was going again, but I didn't care. We were home.

I came in and called Joy.

"The eagle has landed," I said. "And he has some pretty serious tummy trouble. Also, um, the woman I picked him up from . . . I believe is a 'lady of the night.'"

"Is that right?" Joy said. "Well, I could tell you when I talked to her she was higher than a kite."

We spoke a bit about the transport plans. Mr. Man had settled down and seemed to be very sweet so I agreed to keep him until someone could get him out to her in western Pennsylvania.

"What about his name?" I said. "I don't really want to call him 'Mr. Man.'"

"Well, I'd planned to call him Chip after Chipper Jones of the Braves," she suggested.

"Fine, I'll call him Chip." I thought the fact that she was giving him his name boded well for my getting him out of here. "Because he's *your* foster."

She laughed warmly. "I'm looking forward to him."

"He is cute," I said.

"Awwww," she said, her voice like honey. "Poor little darlin'."

I posted a message on the Yahoo! board letting everyone know what was happening. Paul came home from work and Violet came home from being with her babysitter and everyone was happy to see that Chip neither flew nor bit. He was sweet and mellow and deferential to Beatrice so we were all quite happy with him. I spoke to Sheryl the next day and recounted the story. I hadn't had a ton of experience in rescue but I was a fairly experienced dog person and Chip did not strike me as abused, as Coco had said. To say she was an unreliable narrator was fair. The problem was that an accusation of abuse had to be taken seriously. Which I did. And I knew this dog, who was friendly, not hand-shy, and well-mannered, did not have signs of abuse. Joy and I discussed the very distinct possibility that Coco might have some transference issues.

We all agreed very quickly that Chip was a nice dog

(and by "we all" I mean Paul, Violet, me, and the guys who worked in my building—Jimmy, Carlos, Victor, Anthony, Raphael—who became something of an informal approval committee). They were always offering assessments of the new fosters—rating based on personality and appearance. We also all agreed that Hank had set the bar very low; still, Chip was sweet and I had more than a fleeting thought that maybe we would foster him and not send him to Joy after all.

On his first morning while he ate a breakfast of rice and boiled chicken, I looked through descriptions of missing Boston terriers to see if anyone had reported him. There was nothing online. I walked him and Beatrice over to a nearby vet and had them scan his microchip for me. They were able to tell me the registered number and which company's chip it was so I'd know whom to call. I phoned when I got home and they were able to trace it to a large pet chain in New Jersey. Whoever had bought Chip had not changed the contact information. The pet chain, though, had the name, address, and telephone number for the person who bought him. It had been a little over a year and I knew he'd been missing for a while. He'd been with the guy who lived with his mother for over a month before he'd gone to Coco for a couple of weeks. I sent an e-mail to the board of directors telling them about the info I had and Sheryl said she would call the people and inquire about how the dog had been lost, what they'd done to find him, etc. . . . before we would return him. We were all still being cautious because of the original "abuse" report from Coco. After all, the rescue group didn't know me that well and didn't want to risk giving a dog back to an abusive home.

Sheryl had called a few times that day with no answer and no machine and she was so busy with the rest of the rescue group and her own job and life, it seemed to make sense for me to keep calling. I programmed the number into my cell phone and called over and over for the next two days. I double-checked the phone number with information and then called the pet store again. The number I had was correct, but no one had any further word. I checked with my friend Jancee, who is from New Jersey, and she told me the area of New Jersey where the people lived was a nice, pleasant suburb. I put the address into Google Earth and found their house had a small yard. I couldn't zoom in enough to see if there was a fence. A week into the search, it was pretty clear that the people were gone, moved or whatever, and we decided that we'd send them a letter and then we'd know we'd made every attempt to get in touch and would assume Chip into foster care, which at this point we decided would be me. There were so many new dogs coming in and someone had just surrendered two dogs together that Joy could take if I kept Chip.

I e-mailed the progress reports to the board. Some felt the fact that the people hadn't reported the dog missing to the local shelter or to the microchip company showed they weren't really looking and we shouldn't put ourselves out trying to get him home. Sheryl worried, though, that Chip was some little child's best friend and for that possibility we needed to make every effort. I agreed.

I sent my letter and heard nothing for another week. I started to make arrangements to get Chip neutered, a necessary step before reviewing applications. I'd also been feeling a little pull to keep him. He had a wonderful, sweet quality and a very cute personality. Physically he looked like most of the dogs that came into rescue: a little too big with a nose that was a little too long to be considered breed standard. The majority of people who bought $2,600 show-quality Bostons did not lose them or turn them over to rescue.

Coming home from the gym two weeks after I'd picked him up I looked at my cell phone and was about to delete the New Jersey phone number when I decided to give it one last try.

A woman answered.

"Hello?" I said. "I'm calling from Northeast Boston Terrier Rescue. Did you lose a dog?"

"Yes," she said a little unsurely.

"I've got him," I said proudly. "You can come get him."

I heard her say, "Someone has Shaggy!"

She came back on the line. "Where are you?"

"I'm in Manhattan."

"Oh no, that's very far from us. We're in New Jersey."

I didn't respond. My thought was if my dog turned up in Russia I'd be there. She was talking to whoever was in the room. She got back on the phone and said. "Can you mail him?"

I thought about hanging up right then but I just decided to stay with it. "You can't mail a dog."

"Oh," she said wistfully.

"Listen," I said, "I've been taking care of your dog for two weeks. If you don't want him back, that's fine, we can keep him."

She asked me for my phone number and said her husband would call me back. I came home and immediately e-mailed the board. Mary Lou, who I'd learned was the toughest board member, shot back, "Mail him? She's too stupid to get this dog back. If she calls, tell her you are sorry but you lost him again." Everyone was a bit puzzled by the whole thing. I assumed I wouldn't hear from the owners again, and was surprised a bit later when I was in the playground with Violet and my phone rang with their number. It was the husband.

I told him what I'd told his wife, and he told me they'd been in Portugal for the last month. The dog had been lost for three months. He asked me where I lived and said he'd be there in an hour, that he knew how to get to New York City because he had worked at Ground Zero. I gave him directions and told him to call my cell phone when he got into the neighborhood and I'd bring the dog downstairs to the park near my home. By then Paul would be home from work so he could come with me, in case there was any funny business.

A few minutes later the husband called again and apologized for the earlier confusion. He said his wife didn't understand and I wasn't sure but it sounded like she thought I'd stolen the dog and was calling for ransom, hence the comment about mailing him. . . . Still didn't make any sense. I also asked him how Shaggy had gotten lost and he said, "A hole in the fence."

"I hope you've fixed it," I said.

We came home and had dinner and felt a little sad that Chip would be going. We also felt sad that his name was really Shaggy because that was such a stupid name. When the phone rang right around when it was supposed to, I told the guy we'd bring him down. It had started to rain a little, but Violet wanted to go so we put her in her little raincoat and put on Chip's leash.

We could see the father, a daughter, and a small son at the corner across the street. The little boy was jumping up and down. Then I cried. Chip/Shaggy dragged us to his family and jumped up on the little boy—this was what Sheryl had predicted, exactly. The sister produced documents to prove that he was theirs, which I didn't look at. I gave them the leash and we all said good-bye to Chip. The father pressed a one-hundred-dollar bill into my hand and when I refused he said, "Please, it would've cost me thirteen hundred dollars to replace him!" I took the money to send to Sheryl and told him once again to fix the hole in his fence.

We were all happy for the sake of the kids. The parents were clearly not dog people but they loved their children, and their children loved their dog.

If I hadn't trusted my instincts, the story would have ended in a very different way. I don't really know why, but my default setting when I have a sense about anything is "I'm probably wrong." "That guy wasn't lying to me." "That woman isn't on drugs." Part of it is a desire to see people as they appear, because the alternative is so gross. But it's also a leap to trust that you see something that isn't there. I know it would have been more difficult to return Shaggy to his family if Coco had been more credible, but there it was. And that gave me the confidence to listen to instincts the next time something smelled funny, and it would. You have nothing else to rely on when you're dealing with dogs.

LESSON FIVE

How to Be an Amateur Therapist

After Hank and Chip, Violet said she didn't want to help any more dogs. It was confusing and upsetting for her to see these dogs come in and out of our lives. Paul felt the same way, and he became insistent in a way he rarely did. "This is too hard on all of us," he said. "You need to find another way to help these dogs."

Violet also was about to start pre-kindergarten, which would be a full day of school after having spent four straight years pretty much alone with me.

I worried so much about separation issues, just as I had with Otto. But Violet seemed pretty excited about going to school. I realized later, though, that she was under the impression that I'd be going there with her—all day, every day.

I told Sheryl we would be taking a break from fostering, but I'd been talking to Gilda, the transport and home check coordinator, about helping her. The home checks weren't that difficult; when a new application came in, you looked at where the person lived and hoped we had a volunteer close by who would be able to visit the potential home. The transport issue was a whole other big can of slimy worms. It involved arranging the pickup of a dog from a shelter, puppy mill, or home and getting it to a foster family, which could be eight hours away. When I first started, the transports were easier to arrange, but as gas prices started to increase, it became much more difficult to get someone to commit to driving four hours, so we'd have more people driving shorter distances. Coordinating it was something akin to a relay race over several states with a freaked-out dog instead of an egg in a spoon. I helped out as best I could, and then Gilda asked me to take over while she moved to a new home. I agreed, as long as the dogs weren't coming to my house.

I really had my mind focused on Violet. On the first day of school, the kids went for about two hours. Most of the parents looked at it as an opportunity to get some errands done, but I sat outside the classroom with knots in my stomach. It went okay. The next day was three hours, then four, then a full day. The addition of each consecutive hour brought more anguish to my child. I sat in the dimly lit hall outside her classroom. The school was built in the 1920s; it was a grand, Gothic structure with enormous windows and high ceilings in the classrooms. It felt like a real school. In fact, I was reading Frank McCourt's *Teacher Man* while I waited for her and his descriptions of the first schools he taught in in Manhattan and the Bronx sounded very much like this place.

I thought a lot about how I was not able to give Violet the same choice I gave Otto. She had to go to school. Well, she didn't *have* to go to pre-K, but my sense was that if we pulled her out because she was sad and missing me, kindergarten, which was required, would be that much harder.

I thought about a day when I had been trying to teach Otto manners. He developed this habit of barking like crazy at other dogs, or not barking at them and waiting for them to smell him; then he'd try to bite them. I hated saying, "My dog's not friendly," so mostly I'd just pull him away. Initially, though, it was a shock to me. Every time he did it, I thought it was an aberration, there was something provocative about the particular dog he was biting; it was not his fault. But then I started getting it, that he was the one with the behavioral issue. So I had one of my talks with him.

"Listen, you have got to get it together. You're not going to have any friends! No one's going to want to hang with you.

They're already starting to think you're a jerk. It's not my problem, it's yours! If you don't want to behave, you're going to be the one who is embarrassed out there in the world." I used every psychological trick in the book. No little dog was smarter than me! In the end, he decided he preferred his method of communication, and I was right. No one invited him to any of the big doggie birthday parties.

With Violet, it was different. (Strange, but true!) I had a greater responsibility for developing her social and emotional skills. Otto would never be going places without me, but we assumed, one day, that Violet would.

By the Monday after the first easing-in week, my daughter's response to my leaving her at school was no less dramatic than the climactic scene in *Sophie's Choice*. In Violet's four-year-old mind, I was leaving her. Plain and simple. She cried and clung to my leg so that the teacher had to pry her off me and hold her, and then I would leap out, as the assistant shut the door behind me to keep her from escaping. I walked down the hall as her screams echoed, *"Noooooooo!!! Moooooooommmmmmmmmm! Please!!!!!!!!"*

First she had gotten upset when we arrived at the classroom, and the next day she worked her way back to getting upset when we arrived at the school, then when we walked up Broadway, then when we were leaving the apartment, waking up, the night before, etc. . . . When I got her to school, the kids looked at me like I was dropping off a wild thing. They stared at us as they settled into their puzzles and counting games. Those first few weeks, the teacher wouldn't put her name on her cubby because she didn't think Violet was going to stay in the class. For me and for Violet, getting her to school was the hardest thing we'd ever had to do.

The teacher suggested having Paul take her, since maybe she wasn't attached to him in the same way and he could just leave her. On the day we decided to try this method, they left and all was quiet. All morning I didn't hear a peep from him, so I figured the drop-off must have gone smoothly. At around noon he called me from his cell phone. He was *just leaving school.* He actually did worse than I did. So the task went back to me.

When it was clear that she was going to school whether she cried or not, Violet settled in and became a model student, which for pre-K pretty much means not biting or spitting (and for this she won Student of the Month for September!). I happily turned my attention back to rescue.

I arranged my first transport for a sweet, senior Boston named Daisy. She was coming from Somethingsburg, Pennsylvania, and ending up in Nowheresville, New York. I figured it out on Google maps and set a plan into motion; it would kick off Saturday starting at 7 A.M. Friday night we were sitting down to dinner and I got an e-mail. Subject: PROBLEM

WITH DAISY'S TRANSPORT. It seemed that the mother-in-law of the guy lined up to drive the third leg of the trip on the New Jersey Turnpike was in the hospital. The third leg was the hardest to fill, so unless Daisy was hiding her ability to fly, we were going to have to cancel the trip. That wasn't good. Her foster family had worked very hard to find someone willing (and qualified) to adopt this senior rescued dog with a possible two years of life left—condition of that life not guaranteed. If we canceled the transport, we'd lose all of the people who had set that Saturday aside to make that trip.

If I had a car, I'd have driven out there and taken the leg myself. I looked at the New Jersey Turnpike online for the three hundredth time. It seemed like it should have taken about an hour to drive from one end to the other, but that's just not the case. I started walking around in circles, like one of my dogs, and biting my nails.

Paul looked at me with simmering annoyance. Every spare second I was either on Google maps or on the phone with a long-winded volunteer explaining to me all the reasons they couldn't help and how much they wished they could, blah, blah, blah . . . I was screwed. I e-mailed a guy who worked with a neighboring Boston terrier rescue group in Pennsylvania, and he forwarded my e-mail to his transport contacts for other breed rescue groups. One of them e-mailed me back. His name, appropriately, was "Dick" and his e-mail address was Poodle911@dick.com. What he wanted to tell me was that I had no idea what I was doing, I didn't know how to go about arranging a transport or contacting "folks who work pretty darn hard at these transports," and that he saw my e-mail signature and maybe I think that I'm sharper than him because I live in New York City, but he and his country friends . . . And then I stopped reading; I didn't have time to be berated by a Dick (though over the next several weeks I composed dozens of choice e-mail responses in my head). I started making calls to everyone I knew and around 1 A.M. I found an angel willing to fill in the final leg even though it meant her only day off from working at Kohl's department store (one of her two jobs) would be spent chauffeuring a dog. I burst into tears from exhaustion and relief. Not for myself, but for Daisy, whose elderly owner had gone into an assisted living facility. Daisy, who'd had one happy home her whole life and was now on to the third one in a month. And as I got into bed I said, "I'm never doing this again!"

Paul, who had been asleep facing away from me, said, "Yes, you will."

"Then," I responded, "you have permission to kill me."

In between the rescue adventures, I felt so elated not to be fostering or figuring out a transport that it gave me the illusion that my normal life was better than it actually was. It was calm, quiet, with just one little dog. I kept up with the

Yahoo! group, but my work had gotten particularly busy so I was less available.

One day I read a post from Jane, the intake coordinator. It listed several different incoming dogs that I wasn't going to foster—it also mentioned an unknown number of Boston terriers being surrendered by a guy who lived in Washington Heights. He had six dogs, was on disability and welfare, and he just couldn't physically or financially care for them. His social worker was the one trying to get it arranged and wanted to get it done in a hurry, before the guy changed his mind. Since I considered Manhattan my territory, I offered to get the dogs and then whoever was fostering could pick them up from me. We all agreed and then I didn't hear about it for a while. Until Jane called me.

"The gentleman is ready to surrender two of the dogs and we have two foster homes lined up," she said. "Would you like to call him and make the arrangements?"

"Sure," I said.

"He talks a lot," Jane said. "He had me on the phone for a good hour."

"What's wrong with him, do you know?" I asked. "I mean, why is he disabled?"

She didn't know, but she was very relieved when I said I'd communicate with him. His name was John and he was waiting for my call.

I hate talking on the phone. The only time I talk on the phone is on my cell phone when I'm walking somewhere; otherwise I'm an e-mailer. Knowing that I had to call a yapper was making me nervous, so I did what I do when I want a call to be short. I stood up and put on my coat.

I dialed and did a dance of joy when his machine picked up. "Hi, John, this is Julie from NEBTR. Just want to talk about arranging—"

"HELLO, JULIE? I'M HERE!"

No! I'd been so close! He picked up and then I heard the telltale signs of someone settling in for a long conversation—the scraping of a chair, the "hold on while I turn this down," the pouring of a beverage.

John didn't care if I was standing or hanging by my toes; he was going to tell me the long story of his life in three acts, with no intermission.

I heard about his childhood around the corner from where he lived now, as a devoted son and student at Our Lady of Boston Terriers. He was a very successful party planner who knew all the famous people and, "Life, Julie, was good." He took forty minutes to explain this.

Then, he continued, not so good. He bought a female Boston terrier puppy for his mother, and she named her Rachel. And then his mother died. So of course he took Rachel. Then he bought a male puppy for his lover, who named him Pedro, and shortly after that, his lover died, and John took in Pedro. "And then I stopped buying dogs for people!" he said. Then John got sick and lost his job and now he was on welfare. In the meantime, no one ever had Rachel or Pedro neutered. One night Pedro had a couple of drinks and Rachel looked good and the next thing John knew, Rachel was having puppies. So six dogs were all living with him and his roommate (an unrelated person renting a room from him), and he was going to court for some reason, after which he'd have money, but right now he was flat broke and needed our help. Other than his being very long-winded and crying too much, I liked John. I asked him if he wanted to bring the two dogs down to me.

"What? Today? Oh, no, that's too soon." I made him cry. "I need time to say good-bye."

"Okay," I said. "Next week?"

(*Dogs barking.*) "SPARKY!!! *¡Cállate!*"

"It'll have to be before next weekend because I'm going to Puerto Rico [he pronounced it *Pwayrdoh Dreeko,* as if he were a native, even though he was of Greek descent and from New York]. . . . It's my birthday and I'd rather have less dogs here for my friend to watch."

"Uh, okay. Bring them whenever you want."

"I can't bring them to you! I can't afford that!"

Ah, yes. He was going to Puerto Rico for his birthday but he couldn't afford cab fare to my apartment.

"I'll pick them up, then," I said. "Tell me when."

He took a deep, exasperated breath, indicating that he was having a little trouble with my lack of sensitivity and my rushing him.

"Okay, why don't you let me know when you're ready," I declared.

(*Tears again.*) "I'm sorry! This is just very hard for me." (*Dogs barking.*) "FRANKIE, SHUT UP!" (*Back to tears.*) "I'm just. . . . I'm doing the best I can." (*Dog barking escalates.*) "FRANKIE!!! FRANKIE!!!!!"

"I'm going to let you go. I'll speak to you next week." I hung up the phone with a swell of relief. My therapist had many times suggested I'd be good at her job, but I didn't think I could handle it. Ever. I've realized that I can be very good at helping other people with their problems, but I just don't want to get deeply involved unless they're family or friends. John was like a giant octopus with all the arms and suckers trying to pull me into his maelstrom. So I put on my imaginary space suit to keep John at bay.

The plan for the John situation was that a new foster volunteer named Jen would pick up the two dogs from him, but I would meet her there to help her with the surrender.

A flurry of communiqués went between Jane, John's social worker, and me. The social worker was really hoping we could get more than the two dogs—especially since John thought Rachel *might* be pregnant again. (In other words, she was.) I did a lot of oy-veying to Jane, and now Mary Lou was involved because she had had litters of puppies before. We all thought it would be best if when I went to John's, I took a look at the other dogs and the female to assess the situation. I didn't know what to look for in a "pregnant bitch," as they kept calling her, but I thought I'd be able to tell if she was unwell.

We were finally set for a Saturday morning. I'd meet Jen at John's at 9:30. She'd be coming in and taking both dogs, keeping one and meeting up with the other foster family to drop off the other.

On the subway up to John's, I thought about his pups. What if one of them was like Otto? I'd have to take it. What would I tell Paul? The dog had glue on it that attached itself to me. It would be temporary. I got to the station stop in about ten minutes. Being unfamiliar with the neighborhood, I'd printed out a map. I turned onto John's block and was looking down at the map trying to figure out if the building would be on the north or south side of the street when I heard his voice. "JULIE! UP HERE!" I looked up and saw a ripe, round face in a window. "STAY THERE. I'LL BE RIGHT DOWN!"

This neighborhood, Washington Heights, had been quite desirable years ago. My mother's grandmother had lived nearby. The buildings were large, prewar, and built for living. In the 1970s many of them fell into disrepair and stayed there while crime statistics escalated. There had been a recent resurgence of interest in the area and it was now on the upswing, but many parts of it were still stuck in the gloom. This was one of those buildings. It had a small plaza with benches and the front door was now glass and aluminum and locked, though I imagined in the 1940s there had been a uniformed doorman and a fine awning.

I had worn a hooded sweater and a down vest so I could have the extra pockets but, as it was right by the Hudson River, it was cold and *King Lear* windy. I put my hood on and tightened it and stood against the wall for warmth. I waited and looked at my watch and tried the front door and waited some more. It was 9:35 and there was no sign of Jen. I called her on my cell phone and she was stuck in traffic on the George Washington Bridge, which I could see from where I stood. Had it been moving she'd have been there in seconds.

The dogs we were getting were two of Rachel's puppies, Sparky and Pepito. Everyone is always kind of excited when we get puppies because even though they're untrained, they tend to be very little and cute.

The door opened and closed several times before I saw John. He was a heavyset, balding man with a great walrus mustache. He wore khakis and a gray crewneck sweater. In one hand he held a bag of toys, in the other, the leashes. The puppies were about forty pounds of writhing, screaming, biting, and barking. Pepito tried to bite me several times and Sparky just cried. John alternately shouted at them and hugged them, calling them in baby talk "little mushes" and "bacciagalupe."

Here I was, the "expert," and I was at a total loss. We walked the mongrels over to a nearby park, where the wind picked up and a small part of me hoped the two of them would get swept away on a current, two raging kites. No such luck. We talked and waited and every so often I got a call from Jen telling me she'd moved a quarter of an inch. "Well, we're here waiting," I said, remaining upbeat. This was Jen's first foster so in my head I chose Sparky for her, the less terrifying of the two evils.

John regaled me with stories of walking his six dogs, which I could not imagine, these two and *four more*. As we waited the dogs settled down and eventually we hopped up on a stone wall and each held a dog in our lap.

"See what I mean? They're just little loves!" he said while

Pepito licked his face. I wasn't convinced. I had frozen at this point after twenty minutes in the chilly wind, and I guessed the dogs might just be too cold to be bad by now.

John really was a sweet guy. When he told me his lover had died and that he himself was so sick he was on disability, I thought it was something like cancer. Then he started telling me about the court case with his landlord. His apartment was infested with roaches and he'd been *bitten* by them and had been sick ever since. Though I'd lived in Manhattan for twenty years, I had to admit I'd never heard of a person being bitten by a cockroach to the point of disability (or at all—cockroaches bite?). The whole image of the apartment overrun with man-eating cockroaches made me think Sparky and Pepito might have been victims of circumstances.

Jennifer finally rolled up in an SUV driven by her dad. She opened the way back and there were two crates. I had John sign the surrender forms quickly. He didn't bother filling in the information—they had no vets, they'd never had shots. He'd already told me the food they were used to: Doritos, vanilla ice cream, and the #7 from China Fun.

I held the leashes while he picked up each dog. Tears rained down his face into his bushy mustache like the doorman at Emerald City. He held Sparky first, whispered something to him, put him in the crate, and said good-bye. Then it was Pepito's turn. I was sobbing right along with him.

He turned and walked away and I told him I'd call him. He silently waved, and Jen closed the back of the truck and drove off. I walked to the subway trying very hard to get ahold of myself, but it was no use. So I called Paul as I walked.

That night there was a flurry of calls. Pepito was terrifying his foster family and Sparky wasn't faring much better. Jen said she would get a trainer in to work with Sparky but the people who had Pepito didn't even want to go near him. One of the volunteers picked him up and a transfer was made to another foster home. As of this writing, both dogs are still in foster care. They are, in a word, unadoptable.

I had a lot of phone conversations with John, who wanted to know how Sparky and Pepito were doing. I kept my responses vague. He wanted the phone number of the foster family so he could call up and talk to the dog. ("Just have them hold the phone near them. I'll say *puppy, puppy, ice cream.*") He'd signed them over to us and couldn't get them back—as he threatened—if he didn't like what was happening. The social worker was concerned now that it was clear to all that Rachel was going to give birth again. John wanted me to dog-sit for him while he was in *Pwayrdoh Dreeko*. I said, "No way." He wanted Rachel to be somewhere safe in case she gave birth because his roommate wouldn't know what to do. In all the confusion of the pickup, I'd never gotten to look at Rachel, either, to see if she was okay.

I called Mary Lou. "If a dog of mine is going to give birth, I don't go on vacation!" she said. Now, though, apparently John was not going to Puerto Rico for a *vacation*; he was picking up some medication for some elderly neighbor who didn't have a passport, he said. We were all getting a little irritated with John's complete lack of responsibility and the stories and excuses that would continuously morph at a dizzying rate into whatever he needed. And suddenly he was acting like we were his private Canine Staff. We all wanted to make sure the birth went okay, and it wasn't going to help Rachel stay healthy if she was eating Doritos and ice cream. Sheryl and I discussed the appropriate boundaries. I said I'd bring him supplies, healthy food and vitamins and something to use as a whelping box for the birth. I went to my favorite local pet store, Petqua, and picked up a large metal crate, some fifty-pound bags of food, and Nutri-Cal, a vitamin paste. I told the owner the whole story and he said he'd throw in extra samples of food for them. And since I wasn't going to be able to carry it up on the train, I had them deliver it. I also asked him to peek in at the dogs to see if everyone looked okay.

When I came home there was an e-mail forwarded from the social worker who said that I shouldn't be offended that John hadn't invited me in. He probably wouldn't want me in the apartment because of the condition (oh right, the rabid roaches!), and she said when she'd gone there herself her coat smelled so terrible from just being inside that she had to have it dry cleaned—twice.

I was on the phone with John ten times a day. He wanted to know where the food and whelping box were. When were they going to be delivered? Did these people know he wasn't paying? And on and on and on. He had a friend visiting from Europe who was going to stay and watch all of the dogs while he was away. On one of our phone calls, John had just come back from a housewares store to get a "cozy" for the toaster because the friend was a little grossed out by the roaches that were crawling in and around there. John was opening the bag while I was on the phone. He was cracking up at what the guy in the store gave him. "What is this? A *yarmulke*? This isn't going to cover the toaster!" John was laughing but his friend was not. I think I would've been crying.

He had called to say he'd gotten the delivery and that the guys from the pet store were cute. "They're a couple," I said. "Forget it." He laughed. I stopped by the pet store the next day to thank them and ask if they'd gotten a glimpse of the dogs. They said he came out into the hall; they couldn't see into the apartment, but the dogs who came out with him looked fine to them.

I told John that now that this part was over and we were on to puppy-birth phase, he should call Mary Lou with any questions or problems. And as endearing as I found John, I hoped our time together was done.

I very happily heard nothing from him over the next ten days and then one morning I woke up and there were messages on my home and cell voice mail. It was John's number on the caller ID. He was yelling hysterically that Rachel was giving birth at four in the morning and she ate one of the puppies! It was about 7 A.M. and I didn't really know what to do. I Googled "mother dog eat puppy" and learned that when a puppy is stillborn or sickly, the mother dog will eat it so it won't attract predators. It always kind of shocked me when these little pet shop dogs in their Burberry trench coats acted like wolves in the wild. The phone rang and it was John again and he was calmer. Five puppies had been born altogether (including the one she ate). I told him what I'd read and said I'd ask my rescue friends about it. He said they were very cute, and one was brown with blue eyes, and I had to come see them! I really wanted to, but the smelly twice-dry-cleaned coat and the roach thing kind of paralyzed my desires.

I stopped hearing from John and patted myself on the back for a job well-done. Every so often I'd see his name on my caller ID, but he didn't leave a message. I called him back once to check in, but he wasn't there.

Eight weeks after Rachel gave birth I heard from John

again. It was a message on my machine. Through the wailing I heard something about "Rachel" and "murdered." As I was listening, the call waiting rang and it was Mary Lou. She'd spoken to John. He had recently gotten a new roommate and while John was out of the apartment, the roommate claimed Rachel had attacked him and he killed her. He kicked her to death. The cops came and arrested the guy and the DA was up there now. Mary Lou's husband was a New York City cop, and he was looking into it. She said John wanted me to go up there but she told him I was away. It really did feel like lightning just kept striking John. Another friend in the group went to John's apartment and our group arranged for Rachel's burial. It really was a sickening event. Boston terriers aren't killers and nursing mothers are weaker still.

I was at the airport a few months later when I picked up the *New York Post*. There was a picture of John along with the graphic story of Rachel's slaying and the indictment of the roommate for aggravated cruelty to animals.

I resolved to help John when I returned, smelly apartment or not. So often these sweet little needy pups that I desperately want to help are attached to humans who may see this as an opportunity to get some rescuing for themselves. Letting that stand in the way only hurts the dogs. It's always hard to set boundaries, but it's imperative to do it with people you're helping out so you don't go crazy. It's why my therapist doesn't give me her vacation house number. (Why? I wouldn't bother her. Maybe just a quick check-in to see if she's got good weather . . .)

The point is, since rescuing these dogs, on a given day I have anywhere from four to sixteen feet walking all over me. I don't really want any more.

LESSON SIX

How to Fall in Love . . . Again

My life always operates at two speeds, a *Wizard of Oz* cow-in-the-air-tornado velocity and just above flatlining. And now I was in the latter. Work was at a point where I was mostly waiting for things. Violet was settled into her pre-K program. I wasn't sure what I was going to do next and my mind needed occupying.

I had been monitoring the message boards as usual. Since I'd joined the rescue group, I'd heard a lot about a group of surrendered Bostons that became known as "the PA dogs." A family in Pennsylvania had two "intact" (not spayed or neutered) Bostons and their seven puppies. They lived in a trailer and from what I had heard, it was not in good shape.

Apparently their neighbors didn't like that or them, so they demanded the family get rid of all but two dogs. They surrendered five to NEBTR half a year before I joined and everyone who'd fostered one had ended up keeping him or her. They were legendary, the greatest dogs ever. My friend Joy had one, and she occasionally asked Jane and Sheryl if there had been word on the surrender of the final two. She wanted to get them, check out the family, and find out what sort of magical people had created this pack of amazing canines.

Jane called to check in with them and they said yes, they were ready to go. Joy immediately volunteered to pick the two up. One foster home was lined up and they needed another. Joy would forward me all the postings, and gently try to persuade me to consider fostering one. She knew I wasn't that interested in fostering, but she felt one of these dogs would come to us and maybe stay. There were no photos of them, which was my usual method of swaying Paul. It was very hard to look into the eyes of a soon-to-be homeless dog and say, "Nah." Jane posted the little information she was able to glean from the owners. One dog was fine, a sweet fellow. The other one spent his life under the family's couch, terrified by the other dogs. The easygoing dog had a foster home lined up, but the frightened one was up for grabs.

I was wary; I knew that scared dogs could be very tough to take on. The term "fear biter" came to mind. These were timid dogs who lashed out when threatened. Paul and I talked it over and decided we'd try to foster him, but that at the first sign of aggression, he'd have to go elsewhere. We weren't going to be held captive like we had been with Hank. And, no matter what, we were not keeping him. After our brief experiences having two dogs, we realized we didn't want it to be a permanent condition after all.

There was a flurry of correspondence regarding the transport. No one could do the last leg, and in the end, my aunt Mattie offered to take me to meet the rescuer in New Jersey and get him. The trip was arranged for Saturday, but it was a Jewish holiday and the family was coming to Mattie's apartment for dinner. The dog would stay overnight with the last driver, and we'd meet them at an exit of the New Jersey Turnpike Sunday morning. While we were at Mattie's, Joy called to tell me he was in the car, and that Rascal was his name. And she told me about the family. They were a very young couple with a small child—she thought around five—walking around in nothing but a diaper. The place was a mess, but they seemed to really love their dogs. After I spoke to her, she e-mailed me a picture of Rascal. He had a half-black and half-white face. Very cute and solemn, no goofy tongue lolling. I showed the picture to Paul, and Mattie said, "What's that?" And Paul replied, "Our new dog."

Paul and I are partners and best friends, and every other

cliché about a happily married couple, but every time an opportunity with one of these dogs reared its head I would let him know and then wait. I never wanted to push or insist we take a dog. I was willing to do the extra work and bear the bulk of the responsibility but I needed his support to do it. And every time I'd be newly gobsmacked when he said yes. Sometimes I'd be looking at the rescue website and I'd forward him a posting; other times I'd just leave the posting open on my computer. He might not say anything at all, but a day or two later he'd ask, "Did they find anyone to take 'poor old Travis'?"

"I don't think so," I'd say benignly.

And I'd see him wrestling with the idea. He was every bit as much of a softie as I was or more so. The dogs would always win him over.

It was all the more gratifying because Paul hadn't been a dog person when he met me. My first meeting with Paul was when he was interviewing me for a job on the TV show he produced. At the end of the interview, when he asked me if I had any questions, I said, "Can I bring my dog to work?"

"No!" he said.

"You don't like dogs?" I asked, trying to figure out where he was going to land in my book of people.

"It's not that I don't like them," he said unconvincingly.

"I just don't think they belong in an office where people are trying to work."

"Oh."

Later when we started dating, I told him how I felt about Otto and then I got a sense that he didn't love dogs. I was sure, though, that given time, he'd come around to love Otto.

Paul remembers that on our first date he brought a little dog ball as a gift for Otto and I dismissed it, saying that wasn't the kind he liked to play with. After that I felt Paul's resentment toward Otto. He didn't like how I rushed out of work to get home to Otto when he wanted to go have dinner with me. We almost broke up over it, and I'm not exaggerating. I think, then, Paul didn't like Otto. By virtue of being my Otto he was simply in the way. To Paul, I clearly chose Otto's happiness over his own. Maybe I did. I always felt a greater responsibility to Otto because he depended on me for everything. Or maybe it was just my way of expressing what I needed, giving myself space. Working full-time with someone you're dating is pretty intense. Still, I wanted Otto and Paul to like each other. My Zen-like method was to let them both find their way to each other. I wouldn't push it.

Shortly after Paul and I moved in together, he suggested, without malice, that perhaps he (Paul) would sleep on our sofa bed. Otto just took up too much room in the queen-size bed, where he liked to sleep between us with his four stick-straight legs jutting into Paul's back. Then it finally hit me that I wasn't being fair. This was Paul's home and bed, too, and so like my mother did for the dolls that used to crowd my bed at home, I re-created a small version of my bed for Otto right beside me on the floor. His new plush bed came complete with Ralph Lauren comforter. It worked until Paul started to miss Otto and begged him to come back. Otto, in typical magnanimous fashion, humbly relented.

In time, Paul did come around and ended up loving Otto every bit as much as I did. Over the next four years Otto became like our son. Together we came up with dozens of songs about him and no less than forty nicknames of endearment for him. Maybe one or two of them actually came from somewhere, the rest made no sense, but they all meant *"We love you, Otto! You're #1!"* I believe Otto found most of them undignified but tolerable.

Neither of us ever wanted to be away from him. When our wedding was planned in an indoor facility, it was clear Otto wouldn't be there. It was Paul's idea to sculpt a six-inch Otto for the top of the wedding cake. The caterers did a big dramatic unveiling of the dessert table complete with sparklers blazing and the band blaring the cheesy theme to *St. Elmo's Fire*. There in the center of it all atop four tiers of white ganache and several dendrobium orchids perched the clay Otto with a perfect "You've got to be kidding with this" face. Our boy. The guests applauded and cheered. Otto was a hit and he wasn't even there. In my brother Matt's speech, he said, "At one point in about 1996 at the end of a date with a guy who wore a toupee and a fedora, who bowed to Julie while saying good night because he knew he never stood a chance, it was around then that I think she began seeing a face in her mind of a person who she could love." He said, "Before she even met him she knew who this man was, and then she found him, and gave him the name that she'd dreamed of, and that name was Otto."

It once again made me believe that people could change. We both did, because I also tried very hard to stop acting like it was a given that Otto came first.

ON THE WAY to get Rascal, Violet came along when she found out the rendezvous point was a Toys "R" Us, and Bea came along, too, because she loved a car ride. We had just come out of the store, Violet with a new Dora backpack and candy necklace and ring, when we saw the truck pull up with Rascal in the front seat.

I'd done this many times. The dog would jump out, run over, jump up on me, run back, run over to the grass, pee, and eventually would happily hop in the car. Not this time. Rascal, who was so not a Rascal, shook like no dog I had ever seen. Like Scooby-Doo in a haunted house. Though he didn't know the woman who brought him well at all, he Velcroed himself to her leg while she was greeting tiny, perfect Beatrice.

Rascal was twice Bea's size and his markings were all wrong according to breed standard, but he was so, so cute. It was really hard to get him to come over to me, especially with Bea jumping and barking and running around like a lunatic. I finally just took the leash and dragged him into Mattie's car. I held him on my lap; he was just terrified. There is a certain breath I notice my dogs get when they're scared, almost chemical-like, and I smelled it strongly coming from him. At some point in the trip, he relaxed a little and started to release some tension. It was like he let himself get heavier.

The first couple of days I e-mailed with the board, I was of the conviction that this Rascal was irreparably damaged. Sheryl told me what I had told other people: "Imagine how he feels. Give him time."

But it was difficult to have this stricken little fellow who trembled almost constantly and sometimes, like in the elevator, seemed close to passing out from fear. I felt so sorry for him and hated that I just could not get through to him and calm him down.

While Violet was in school I sat with him and talked to him and told him no one would be scaring him anymore. He was safe and loved. After spending some time with him one morning I told Paul I felt strongly that we must change his name. He didn't respond at all to Rascal, and it was just so totally unsuited to him. He was such a serious guy. He struck me more as a Gandhi. I e-mailed Sheryl to say that I would be changing his name, and she said fine as long as I didn't name him Buddy or Buster because the database was overflowing with them. But she should know, *I still wasn't keeping him.*

"What's your name?" I asked him, scratching him behind his ears. He put his muzzle on my lap and from somewhere out in the naming ether it came to me. Moses.

I swear that once he had a new name, his personality changed to go with it. He was a little less nervous, he would let you pet him longer, and wherever I went, he was right there with me. Beatrice was a bit of a loner, so when we were in the apartment she'd be off in our room tucked away in her bed, and Moses mostly had me to himself.

I worried a lot about him. The first two days he did not go to the bathroom at all. I'd call Sheryl while I walked him. "Eventually he will go," she said. "He'll have to." She was right. Finally the third day he peed, one long, long, *long* pee. I didn't know who was more relieved, he or I. I found myself talking about him all the time. A new foster moving in is always dramatic, but he was also so enigmatic. He didn't gobble down food or go crazy when he heard a noise. He was a somber, earnest boy. I reread the original post about how he spent all of his time hiding under the couch, and I planted my lips on the top of his very flat head. While doing the dishes one day, I looked down at him. He was staring up at me and I think from that moment on, his eyes never left me.

He started to come into his own—or as much of his own as he could—at about the one-month mark. I noticed that he didn't shake anymore, and he was absolutely smitten with me. I have to say the feeling was mutual. I would pick him up and put his front legs over my shoulder, his big head right at my face, looking into my eyes, breathing his breath. I would start slow dancing, singing, "Heaven, I'm in heaven . . ." Then I'd dip him. Paul would yell, "Get a room!"

We laughed a lot with Moses. He reminded us of Buster Keaton, all deadpan and black-and-white. And he just blossomed like a sunflower. He got a little skip in his step and just the tiniest amount of moxie. He started to bark at other dogs and wag his tail and chase squirrels and even have a little swagger. The feeling we had of taking this dog from under the couch in the trailer and restoring him to the top of the bed was pretty breathtaking. We were very proud of what he was able to accomplish.

Occasionally, ever so slightly, he bit people. Like when my brother came to visit. Matt strode into our apartment and came to give me a hug and Moses jumped up and bit him on the ass. Matt told me later that the only cure for this type of behavior was euthanasia. I told him I didn't want to make him feel any worse, but I think I'd sooner euthanize him than Mosie. I did have to keep him on a little tighter lead, though. We just had to be extra careful.

So Moses burrowed his way into my heart. I just loved him and it was different from the other dogs. He became my little boy, my fur kid, as Oprah says. He always wanted to be near me. When I worked at the computer, he sat his big body on my lap and put his head on the keyboard. It was okay, I could always use another space in between words. Plus, it represented how far he had come. He had a minor setback when I took him to get neutered. All the shaking came back. But the vet's office was absolutely in love with him, and when I came to pick him up the entire staff came out to say good-bye. About a day later he was okay again.

I loved him to the moon and back. I wouldn't want to compare any other dog, but I did think he was the first dog who came close to being what Otto was to me. I never thought it was possible that once I had an adoring spouse and loving little child, I would still feel the dog love in the same way I did when I was single. But with Moses I began to understand that "dog" was its own category of "love." Sometimes you just need to hold and kiss a member of the dog species. Even when humans are available.

And with that growing connection, Violet started to turn on him. Just four at the time, she asked with increasing regularity if Moses could go live with Paul's uncle Dan, who had often talked to us about getting a dog. And then she stopped asking *if* he could go, and she started pointing at days on the calendar that would be good for him to leave. It reminded me of when my friend Mae had a baby girl. Her son often asked if they could send her back to the sky.

"Mom, Moses isn't going to live here anymore, he's moving away," Violet would announce. "We don't want him here anymore."

"Your Jedi mind tricks won't work with me, kid," I told her. But I tried to make things better. Moses wanted to be the closest one to me. In the evening, Paul and I would read books to Violet before she went to sleep. We would lie on our bed with Violet in the middle of us, but now Moses would jump up and get between her and me. And she'd be shoving him and pushing him and grunting at him to move. He would suction himself to the bed and stare straight ahead as if he were deaf. She grew more frustrated, and he remained stubborn. I wasn't happy that Violet was having difficulty, but I did think that the simulated sibling conflict might not be a bad thing in the end.

Our schedules had gotten busier. Paul's workday was longer now and I was doing all of the household, child, and dog chores. I started to feel like walking the dogs punctuated every moment of my life. It sort of reminded me of breast-feeding, in that I was either doing it or heading toward doing it or just finishing doing it. So we hired a dog walker to do one of the shifts. In the evenings, she came in and sat on the floor leashing up the dogs and talking to them in her funny dog voice. "What is this lady doing to me?" she squeaked, as though she were one of them. "I was just fine sitting here minding my own business. I don't want to put my leg through there! Oh, lady!"

For the sheer fact that she wasn't me or Paul, Moses didn't want to go with her. It was always a struggle. She came in one night upset and said Moses had wiggled out of his harness, but she'd been able to grab him before he went into traffic. I'd never had that problem with him before but we tightened up the harness so it wouldn't happen again.

It was a very chaotic time in our home. I was getting ready for a book publication that involved a tour of eight cities in eleven days. I would also be leaving Violet for the first time in her life, and I'd never even taken an overnight trip away from her. My mother would come to stay with her and Paul and then he'd come out and meet me on the West Coast. We talked about it a lot. I would call all the time, I'd always have my phone with me, and she could have whatever she wanted while I was away. When Paul came to meet me, my mother would take Violet and the dogs up to her house in Vermont, which was near my last tour stop so I'd come and pick her up there. It was so stressful. Not my first book or this development in my life, but abandoning my child. My therapist suggested that this was a good thing for Violet, that she'd probably thrive and would feel very good about herself afterward. It was all being planned and then my dad said no to bringing the dogs up. We'd come there briefly with Moses and Bea at Christmas, and Moses had started fights with my parents' dogs. He just had no good social experience. Bea had taken on being the alpha at home, but elsewhere, to Moses, it was still up for grabs. I understood my father's feelings, that they were going to have to deal with little Violet and maybe that was enough. So I decided on the dog walker coming to our apartment to dog-sit. In a distant second place to my concerns for Violet was my fretting for Moses. How would he take our leaving? Would he think we were gone forever? Would he bond more with the dog walker or totally freak out? Clearly, if there's a more anxious person than me, they are probably sitting in a hospital somewhere. When I finish worrying about one thing, I can go to the list and take my pick of the next.

At the three-week countdown I started physically preparing: ramping up my gym schedule, shopping for new clothes, making hair appointments, figuring out which nail polish would say to people around the country, "I'm a writer you want to get to know better!" It was a lot like my wedding, except that I hoped, in the future, I'd have other books.

In truth, I was excited and happy and felt like for the first time in my life I was realizing myself. I loved my husband, my daughter, my work, and I was in love with a dog again, something I never thought would happen after Otto. With Beatrice I very consciously kept from getting too close to her. I didn't want the heartbreak I had with losing Otto ever again. But Moses blindsided me. He slipped in through an unguarded entrance.

One evening, the dog walker came to pick up Bea and Moses while Violet was taking a bath. As she was playing with the bubbles, she told me she wanted Moses to go away forever and never come back. She had also told me this in the morning. I don't know why but that day he was really getting in her craw. I was used to her insistence.

It wasn't much later when I heard first the house phone and then the cell phone ring. I answered and it was the dog walker and she was upset but I was having difficulty understanding her. I finally heard that Moses had gotten out of his harness.

"Where are you?" I asked.

"In the lobby with Bea," she said. "He ran out the front door before the doorman could shut it. Some men went after him."

I whipped Violet out of the bath and threw clothes on her and we ran down to the lobby. I told the dog walker to take Violet up to the apartment and I'd go look for him. Violet was too upset, though, and she wanted to go. As we were leaving the building, my next-door neighbor and close friend Margaret was coming in and when I told her about Moses, she dropped her bags and went to look with us. It was twilight, and the doorman had seen him go east, so that's the way we went. We got a block away and I realized it was just impossible to try to look for Moses at Violet's pace, so Margaret took Violet back to her apartment. I tried to call the city to see if anyone had reported him, but I couldn't get through, so I called my mother and asked her to keep trying to call the city, and then I called Paul and left a message on his cell phone. I phoned Mattie, who was out to dinner. She said, "He'll come back."

I walked and called his name, thinking of where he could

have gone. I was worried that someone had grabbed him, someone not nice. We were always hearing about people who used small dogs as bait for training pit bulls to fight. I had to stop thinking of that. I worried that he'd gone into Central Park, which was now falling into darkness. I even tried to talk to him telepathically. I felt like I should've been able to figure out where he had gone, but my mind was blank, except for thinking about Moses being afraid. I thought about his eyes and how it felt to hold him and how terribly much I had let myself love him. If he was lost forever, I thought I might go crazy. I felt horrendous anguish and guilt for not having replaced the stupid harness when the dog walker first noticed he could get out of it.

I decided to walk back toward my apartment and go west, look in the park by our apartment building and then head toward Riverside. I walked and looked between buildings and called his name, my voice starting to break. When I got up to my building, a group of guys who worked there and people I didn't know were talking about where they'd looked and who had seen him go. I said I was going to try the other park. It was probably a hundred feet from the door to Broadway, where there are two wide lanes of traffic going north and two going south separated by a median. I looked across Broadway and saw him. I saw his eyes shining and he saw me. I yelled for him to stay, but he didn't. He came toward me and into an oncoming SUV. The rest of what happened operated on some other level of my consciousness, because when that car hit Moses, my thinking stopped and it was all feeling. He lay in the street in a pool of blood, not moving. Before another car could hit him I ran out and picked him up. I could still feel his heart beating, but he had been hit head-on. I was kissing him and crying and neighbors whom I'd never spoken to ran with me up to a vet two blocks away. My mind was replaying and replaying the events of the evening. I wanted to go back so badly and change what had happened that I almost felt I could. When we got to the vet, I was covered in blood and tears. They took Moses into the emergency room, and I sat with these two kind strangers.

"Maybe they can do something," the woman said.

I begged and pleaded with God. Paul called and he couldn't understand what I was saying, and I just told him to come to where I was. A few seconds later the vet came in and said he would not be able to save him, that he'd been hit in the head and it would be better to let him go. I needed to give him permission. He asked me if I wanted to go in and say good-bye, but I had done that when I carried him. I knew he'd had some breath in him, and the last image he'd been conscious of was seeing me across the street and I just tried to stay with that. Paul came in and I told him Moses was gone. We both cried and gathered our things. The neighbors left and we walked home together in pieces.

Unlike when Otto had died, I was now a parent of a small child and I couldn't let myself totally fall apart. When we came home, Violet was still at Margaret's. Margaret came over and without saying a word hugged me and cried. A few minutes later Paul came in with Violet, who did not know what had happened.

"Did you find him, Mom?"

I said no at first, thinking it would be easier for her to think of him as having "run away" than having been killed. And she went into a panic. Of course it had to have been the day she demanded he go away that this happened, and now she thought she had driven him off and she wanted to know why I had stopped looking for him. So I told her that he had gone to heaven, a place she was somewhat familiar with. Paul's parents were in heaven, and his uncle had recently moved there.

Now my little girl was so hurt and crying and crying. She said she was sorry, and if she was sorry, could he come back? Paul and I told her that it was an accident and none of it had anything to do with her. She lay down on our bed weeping until she fell asleep.

I e-mailed Joy and told her. She posted on the message board:

Hi All—

This is probably the most difficult post I've ever made.

Julie Klam's beloved Moses (one of the PA Dogs and my Cal's littermate) somehow got out of his harness today while being walked by the dog walker. He was loose in Manhattan for over an hour. Julie chased and chased him. As he was heading back home, he went to cross a median and was hit by a car. As Julie was taking him to the vet, he left for the Bridge. Fortunately, Violet, Julie's 4-year-old daughter, was taken by a friend and didn't see it. Julie is now explaining to Violet that Moses has gone to doggie heaven.

Please say a very special prayer for Julie and her family and light a candle so Moses can see his way to the Rainbow Bridge.

Hug your pups just a little closer tonight for Moses.

The Rainbow Bridge refers to a poem:

Just this side of heaven is a place called Rainbow Bridge.

When an animal dies that has been especially close to someone here, that pet goes to Rainbow Bridge. There are meadows and hills for all of our special friends so they can run and play together. There is plenty of food, water, and sunshine, and our friends are warm and comfortable.

All the animals who had been ill and old are restored to health and vigor. Those who were hurt or maimed are made whole and strong again, just as we remember them in our dreams of days and times gone by. The animals are happy and content, except for one small thing; they each miss someone very special to them, who had to be left behind.

They all run and play together, but the day comes when one suddenly stops and looks into the distance. His bright eyes are intent. His eager body quivers. Suddenly he begins to run from the group, flying over the green grass, his legs carrying him faster and faster.

You have been spotted, and when you and your special friend finally meet, you cling together in joyous reunion, never to be parted again. The happy kisses rain upon your face; your hands again caress the beloved head, and you look once more into the trusting eyes of your pet, so long gone from your life but never absent from your heart.

Then you cross Rainbow Bridge together. . . .

—Author unknown

We lit the candle, knowing that if there was a heaven for dogs, Moses would be there before too long.

LESSON SEVEN

How to Mourn the Loss of a Friend

As of this writing, my lifetime dog count is seventeen family dogs. Ten during the eighteen years I lived with my parents, and seven dogs with my own family. Seventeen, of which thirteen are gone. Unfortunately "the end" is part of every dog story, and if you have dogs, you have to reconcile with that unless your personal ethics and bank account permit cloning.

When Misty, our standard poodle, died, I was in fourth grade. I made her a wooden grave marker out of a scrap from my father's toolshed, and adorned it with markings from a ballpoint pen. I walked to the woods where she was buried, a place no one ever went to, and there I found the clearing where my dad told me he had buried her. At least I thought that's where it was, and at any rate I dropped the grave marker there and ran really fast back to the house. I didn't want any poodle ghosts after me.

In the fall of seventh grade our great mastiff, Lioness, started having difficulty managing the stairs and then walking at all. Mastiffs are prone to hip dysplasia. I was leaving for school in the morning, following my brothers out the front door, and I turned back and looked at my mom's face. She was crying. On the bus I began to realize that Lioness was at her end, that it was likely going to be her very last day, and that I had not had a chance to say good-bye. When I got to school, I was sobbing and was brought to the guidance counselor, who called my mom. She picked me up and we were both crying. She told me they would be putting Lioness down later that day. I went into the house and found Lioness in her spot, her tail still, not the usual *thump-thump* when we went toward her. I lay down on her and I cried and cried and said good-bye and told her I loved her. I went with my mother to the vet in Pound Ridge where our kind and WASPy veterinarian greeted us in madras pants and a starched white polo. He came out to the car and lifted the rear door of the SUV, where Lioness, prone on a chaise longue cushion, waited. I thought about the time we were at the vet and my mother was laughing so hard she was wiping the tears off her face with her sleeve because the country club vet was treating a white husky named Honky. Now my mother was gulping and biting the inside of her mouth and looking off into the distance, trying not to let the tears flow. Lioness looked briefly at the vet, laid her head down, and closed her eyes. My mother covered her with an Indian print bedspread and closed the door quietly and we drove her home. Sometime later my dad did the job of burying her, driving her to the graveyard behind the tennis court. I don't remember thinking about it after that day.

When my beloved Otto died, I had the time and the space to grieve the way I wanted. I was pregnant, I wasn't working, and I was flagrantly hormonal, so I felt perfectly comfortable walking down the street weeping.

With Moses, I was in a different stage of my life altogether. Though I'd had Otto for seven years and Moses for only three months, Moses had gotten under my skin. In a brief time, he'd become a dog of my heart. But it was just a few weeks before I was going to leave on a book tour, and with a small child in school, I didn't have the luxury of letting it all hang out. I remembered years before asking Paul's mother about how she managed the death of her husband at age forty, suddenly becoming a widow and single mother of four boys. She'd said, "Honestly, I would've liked to crawl under the covers and stay there, but for my kids' sake, I couldn't afford to." She pushed her feelings down and went to work. In no way would I ever compare the loss of a husband and father of your children with the loss of Moses, but I wanted to know how it was possible to cope with a death when you're not at liberty to grieve the way you'd like. So like Paul's mother, I compartmentalized. I had my sadness, but I kept it separate.

As sorry for myself as I felt, my greatest concern was for Violet. The day after Moses's death, she started to say he was just lost. We paid very close attention to her. She would say he was in an accident, and then later, that she hoped we would find him soon. Some days she'd be angry with me for losing him and then ask if we could go back out and look for him. One night as we were going to bed she got herself dressed in her clothes again and wanted to head out and find him. She said she knew where he was.

There was, as there always is, a lot going on in our lives, and plenty of potential distractions for Violet. We focused on Beatrice, telling Violet that Bea needed us to take care of her. But if our apartment door opened and Bea went into the hall, Violet would start screaming. It was a while before she stopped thinking that Beatrice was in danger of going to heaven any second she was out of sight. I knew that kids don't take in what they can't handle, but it was months before Violet finally accepted that Moses was gone. Several months later, she told a friend that he'd gone to live with a new family who had a house and grass.

I was consumed by the vision of Moses's accident. It played on a loop in my brain. Every time I left my apartment building and saw that spot where he'd been hit, I felt distraught and nauseated. I could be shopping, or e-mailing, or working out at the gym and I'd see Moses coming and the car and I'd wince and try to shake the images out of my head. Or I'd press my palms against my eyes as if the picture was "out there" instead of in my brain.

In every way I could, I tried to accelerate the mourning period. Throughout the months that followed, I would think about him and feel a sense of having had something that slipped through my fingers. I felt that I'd lost him too soon. Since I never found the silver lining of the experience, I was somewhat relieved when they paved over the spot where he'd been hit on Broadway.

Being a part of the rescue group helped me immeasurably. It became like a support group. There wasn't a single member who couldn't identify with the depth of my anguish and the fact that it was hard to express to the outside world. Every time someone said they prayed for him or lit a candle, I felt grateful.

Often when I meet people and tell them I have dogs and work with a rescue group, I hear stories of the dog who was, without question, the sweetest, the smartest, and quite simply the best dog who ever lived. If I talk about my dogs, I see a look in their eyes that says, "No, you don't understand, *this dog* was different." And I always understand. That dog *was* different. There are some people who experience the loss of a dog and decide never again to go through that. They don't want to get another dog; they don't want to feel that thing again and have it taken away. There are risks when you love someone and maybe people feel that this is one way they can control it.

Otto's and Moses's deaths were significantly different. Though I was unprepared for both, I don't think the dogs were. I have often felt that dogs know, however they die, that it's coming. Not long ago my parents' beloved golden retriever, Frankie, was hit by a car. It was the kind of accident you feel should not have happened. They were going for a walk, the same walk they'd done every day for the six years they had him. He was already on the other side of the road and they heard a truck coming, so my dad called the dogs. Frankie, ever obedient, just came bounding into the road without looking. He never knew what hit him.

Later when we talked about it, my mom said she felt Frankie had been acting strange all day. "There was something going on with him," she said with certainty. And their other dog, Peaches, didn't have much of a reaction to his death. It was like they'd all dealt with it on this higher plane in their magical dog way. If only we were privy to what goes on there. I've always thought that dogs are spiritually superior to humans, which is why I think they have such abbreviated lives. They do their business here on earth and then move on.

Some months ago I was having dinner with a friend of mine, Diane, who lives near me in New York City. We'd actually been to a screening of *Marley & Me* together, and naturally the topic of dogs and death came up. I told her about Otto and Moses and she told me about her son Sam's dog, Radar, who was now in his twilight years. Sam lived in Los Angeles and was grown-up and married, but he'd gotten this dog shortly after her husband had died, when Sam was twenty-two, and they all credited Radar with getting Sam through his father's death. She was very concerned about how devastated her son was going to be when it was Radar's turn—it wasn't something that appeared to be imminent, just inevitable.

I thought about them a lot, Sam and Radar, though I'd never met them. When I walked Beatrice in the park in the mornings, I often ran into a man in his mid-fifties who had an old shepherd mix named Gravely (after the brand of tractor because when he was a pup he'd "mow everyone down"). Gravely was sixteen, which is pretty old for a big dog. He couldn't walk much, so his owner would carry him from Riverside Drive to the park where he'd once run and set him down in the grass. Gravely would take a few tentative arthritic steps and lie down. His owner would stand beside him looking out at the Hudson River. Sometimes I'd come over to pet Gravely and say hello; other times I sensed the man and Gravely needed their privacy. They were going through a process. I didn't see them every day so it took a couple of weeks before I realized they'd stopped coming and I sat in the grass Gravely and his owner had once claimed and said a little prayer for them both.

Not long after Diane told me about Radar, she went to Los Angeles. Something was happening with Radar and she felt she needed to say good-bye to him. Sam assured her there was plenty of time. A couple of weeks later, Sam e-mailed me Radar's heartbreaking obituary.

I have talked so much about dog death because almost every time someone close to me goes through it, the same question comes up: Why is this so hard for me to deal with? A very close friend admitted to me that losing his dog had been harder than losing his loving aged father. Another friend said, "The hardest part is that most people don't understand . . . it wasn't just a dog." There's a framework in place for dealing with human death that doesn't really exist for animal companions. Otto was a beloved friend, but also an incredibly significant comfort to me. He knew when I was sad or worried and often acted it out for me (hiding under the bed and such) and it would help me to cope. I kept thinking how badly I needed him to help me deal with his death.

Everyone talks about it, but animals are so selfless and their love is unconditional. They aren't angry with us for more than a few seconds and their actions don't mask ulterior motives. Well, except for one of my dogs, who pretends to be a good watchdog if he wants something I'm eating. He says, "Woof woof," but means "Look how brave I am; you should give me some of that cheese."

We are responsible for our dogs. It's up to us to figure out when they get walked or vaccinated and what they eat and when (except for garbage; they decide that on their own). We also decide whether or not to put them through chemotherapy. And when the time comes, we decide whether or not to put them to sleep. It's an awesome guardianship to be entrusted with.

That responsibility is not one I take lightly. At best, a dog's life is short, compared to a human's. There was a black Lab in my old neighborhood who died at age twenty-four. The oldest dog ever lived to be twenty-nine years and five months. And that's a part of the human-canine bond we have to reconcile with. When Otto died, I was told by a really wonderful animal communicator that he had work to do on the "other side," namely helping my unborn baby into the world. Somehow that made the task of accepting that he would never get to know my new daughter easier.

AFTER OTTO DIED, I wrote something that was so painfully depressing that I have never been able to read it again. I wanted so much to evoke the sadness I felt and make sure everyone else felt it, too. My fear was that since Otto was a dog, he'd be forgotten. What I wrote emulated the stirring valedictories written for Lou Gehrig, the great Yankee who died at age thirty-nine from ALS. Fitting? I am not sure.

Is that what Otto would have wanted? Would he want me to be morose and sacrosanct? I always listen very closely when someone talks about what they want people to do when they die. "I want everyone to have a big party and laugh and play the *White Album*!" or "I want a small group of my closest friends to tell stories and get drunk." My father doesn't want a funeral; he wants to be cremated and for everyone to just go about their business. My aunt Mattie, on the other hand, has asked my brothers and me since we were kids to promise (and she gives us money when she's saying this) that when she dies, we'll throw ourselves on her grave wailing and sobbing, "Don't go, Aunt Mattie, please don't go!" I appreciate this. Really, I've always agreed with her. When I die, I want people to be sad. Actually, I'd like to have one of those services that are standing room only. (But really I don't want to die.) So my transference with Otto went to the end; I thought he'd want me to mourn him like a Victorian widow.

I wrote back to Sam after I got Radar's obituary, but it wasn't until a long while later that I met him and heard how he was finally able to let Radar go.

One day he had been running a few errands with Radar. The back of his SUV had always been Radar's place, with a bed and toys and treats and water. Now, Sam had to lift him in and out of the car instead of his leaping in and out. Radar's feet were really hurting him at this stage, and walking on concrete was almost impossible. Sam drove past a street lined with lush grass and pulled over to give him some relief (he had to hold him up to use the bathroom at that point). As Radar stood on the grass, not quite feeling like taking any steps, Sam rooted him on and stood, prepared to help. A flatbed truck drove by them, slowed down, made a U-turn, and drove back to where Sam was standing with Radar. A man around age fifty got out and approached them. He asked Sam if Radar was his dog. Sam said yes and the man looked at him with compassionate eyes and said, "I have had dogs all my life, and I currently keep three dogs at home. I drove by and could just tell that you are not seeing the truth in your dog. It is time to let him go. You really have to do the right thing by him now." He got into his truck and drove away.

Later, when Sam told his wife and mom and mother-in-law, they all told him that the man was an angel sent to him. He made the appointment soon after to put Radar to sleep.

Being the one who has to make the choice is a terrible responsibility, and it's almost never as clear as you wish it would be.

A very wise dog woman once told me that dogs find owners, not the other way around. They pick you and they choose to stay with you. In that way, they are also giving you the end of their life. The deeper the bond, the harder it is to say goodbye. I know I'd rather have any amount of time with a dog I love and suffer the mourning than not have the time at all.

LESSON EIGHT

How to Uncover Truths

We had remained committed to our ban on fosters, even though our time with Moses had proven there were potential dog soul mates out there.

About four months after Moses's death, our home was empty of guests, and we were asked to be a layover for a transport of two Boston terrier puppy mixes. I agreed, since it was just a day or two and they were little teeny cute pups. I hooked up with the transport very early Friday morning in Tribeca and picked the little armloads up. They were unsurprisingly cute, and they went by the names of Sarah and Lizzie. We would only have them until Sunday night. Piece. Of. Cake.

You would think that I'd have learned at some point that

nothing involving rescue dogs is ever simple. They were *puppies!!! Unhousebroken!!! Totally destructive!!!* In an hour, one of them had eaten the power cord for Paul's laptop *and* my iPod. The night after they arrived I had to speak to a book club in New Jersey. While I was getting ready to go, Lizzie jumped on our bed and took a pee. I was so insulted and stunned. I took the sheets off the bed while explaining to her that she was a guest in our home and while I didn't expect her to wash dishes, there were some house rules I'd appreciate her following. She walked with me to the washer and dryer and stood beside me as I put the new clean sheets on the bed. I asked her to please leave the bedroom because I would be closing the door with her outside. Unfortunately, I was missing one pillowcase, and I stepped out to the linen closet. By the time I put the pillow on the bed, she'd done it again! She got back on the bed and pissed on the same spot. Twice in five minutes. "Someone is not angling for an invitation back here!" I said.

Paul got home from work early to be with Violet while I went to New Jersey. About every seven minutes my phone rang. It was Paul.

"They are pissing and crapping everywhere!" he said. He didn't expect me to come home; he just wanted me to know what the situation was. And, evidently, make sure I was as miserable as he was. I said I'd clean it up when I got home, and then he called me one final time to say, "Lizzie just pissed on our bed again!"

Three days after they were supposed to leave, Lizzie and Sarah finally left. I wanted to help, but I wasn't sure I could again. I thought it might be better to arm ourselves with another foster, just in case any puppy transports were passing through and looking for a way station. My marriage was strong, but those puppies could chew through anything.

On a crisp April morning, I got an e-mail about a Boston in the Manhattan Center for Animal Care and Control (CACC), the real New York City pound. It was located right across town from me and I was asked to pull him out of there. His foster home was to be determined. Tara, a woman from pug rescue, was the contact. She worked with the shelter and was contacted when pugs, French bulldogs, or Boston terriers came in and then she figured out where they should go. They waited a week to see if anyone claimed him (in this case it was an owner surrender, but the rules stood, I guess in case the dog wasn't really the owner's to surrender). In the meantime, she was going to go and have a look at him and see what he was like. The shelters do an assessment of a dog when he comes in, but they aren't terribly accurate. Imagine if your dog got lost and was picked up by the dogcatcher, brought to a shelter, placed in a cage, and *then* his personality was assessed. The dog is nervous, hyper, hand-shy, aggressive with other dogs, bites, doesn't eat, etc. . . . None of us really pays too much attention to the assessment. Almost every dog that I've gotten from a shelter has been nothing like their description.

I decided to read through the information about him anyway.

The initial intake report said:

SHERLOCK—Six-year-old neutered Boston terrier, OS (owned three years, allergies)—ID HOLD until Sat. April 19. Owner surrender, allergic. Per owners, good with adults and kids, agitated around other dogs.

Shortly after that a volunteer from the shelter met with him. She had this to say:

Sherlock's owner surrendered him, explaining his son was allergic to dogs. But he assured us that Sherlock loves all people, but wants to be the only dog in a household. Sherlock is overweight (at twenty-five pounds, he's really carrying too much weight for his breed). He's very friendly and great on the leash. He has been calm around other dogs, but we'll take his owner's word that he doesn't like other dogs. He is housetrained, has a very good appetite (his weight reflects that fact), and is a cute little guy. He's around ten years old.

Within minutes his age went from six to ten years old. Between perspectives, human error, and the total chaos that is a shelter, color is about the only fact they get right. I'm often amazed I don't end up taking home a zebra.

Tara sent a request to see if the CACC could have a behaviorist evaluate him. It was going to be nearly impossible to find a foster family without other dogs, and the ones with dogs were wary of one who wasn't going to get along well with the home crew. She also offered to come in herself and have a look if that wasn't possible.

The woman at the shelter said probably no to the behaviorist, but she herself had taken Sherlock out with a Chihuahua and he had seemed fine. He was really a sweet dog. Tara decided to go meet Sherlock; this was her report:

> I went to the shelter today and spent some time with Sherlock. Boy, is he *obese*! He is the fattest Boston I have ever seen. He is even fatter in person than he is in the pictures. From his frame, I would guess he should weigh 18–20 pounds, and they said he weighs 25 pounds, which is *a lot* of extra weight! But, he is equally happy and wiggly. He is super sweet—I took him out of his cage and he immediately rolled over for a belly rub! Then I took him outside and played fetch with him for about ten minutes to try to get

him some exercise! He seemed like he had a lot of fun and has a great personality. There was a big rottweiler in one of the pens nearby. Sherlock ignored him until I coaxed him over to say hello. They sniffed each other through the pen, and then Sherlock turned away like he didn't care. I don't see any aggression in him at all! When we went back inside, there was an X-pen of pit bull puppies, and he completely ignored them too.

He is one of the staff favorites. They are tracing his microchip, which is why he is on hold until Saturday. Despite his size, he moves around pretty well and has a lot of spunk in him. Let me know if you are able to find a foster home for him.

Thanks!
Tara

I read this and was laughing so hard Paul came over to see it and then he was laughing, too, and then I e-mailed it to Mattie and she called me up laughing. She also said, "You're going to take him, aren't you?"

"I'm going to pick him up—well, not physically because I don't want a hernia."

The fat jokes were rolling!

SHERYL HAD WRITTEN BACK to Tara that it was as she had suspected, that the personality information had just been misleading. She also wanted to see if Tara thought the dog was six or ten.

Tara wrote:

> Of course, as with any dog, the foster home should use caution. But I didn't see anything to be concerned about. It will depend on the other dogs in the home as well.
>
> If I had to guess, I would have said eight years old. But with a little TLC (nail trim, bath, and losing five pounds) he will look much younger. He has a bit of gray on his face, and his teeth had a decent amount of tartar. He certainly ran around like he was a six-year-old dog, and once he loses weight he will run around with more ease. I just don't think he was taken care of as well as he should have been.
>
> He is super sweet though! Right now, the shelter has him slated to leave under my name (assuming no one claims him). If you find someone and they are going to pick him up, just let me know and I will tell the shelter that person's name. Doesn't make a difference, as long as he gets out of there.

> Keep me posted and let me know if I can help. I would take him myself if I didn't *still* have this French bulldog!!!

It was always significant to me when a volunteer said they'd take a dog if they could. I met a lot of dogs and didn't want them all. Paul and I talked a little about it. We thought the potential comic aspects of Sherlock would be great and didn't think it sounded like he could do any significant damage, especially if he couldn't move that much.

I read under the note for me to pick him up that they still needed a foster home to get him started on a new, thinner life. I told Sheryl that I would pull him and foster him. We were all excited. We waited to get the call that he was free to leave.

It took a week. Saturday night they said he'd be available for pickup anytime after 9 A.M. on Sunday, so we planned to go then. After breakfast and walking Bea, we boarded the crosstown bus.

The shelter in East Harlem was not as bad as some of the others, though the relentless sounds of barking made me feel ill at ease. It always felt insignificant to be taking one dog when there were so many more. And usually we would be taking the most adoptable one—a lovely purebred Boston terrier. Small dogs and purebreds are the most desirable at a pound, especially in New York City.

We arrived and were sent back to the offices of New

Hope, the group who works with rescues. The contact, Lisa, was waiting for us. She told us to fill out a form and she would get Sherlock. She came back in with the handler, and when I first saw him the word "manatee" came to mind. He had a tiny (or was it just regular-sized?) head on this huge body. He also had Bordetella, or "kennel cough." So he was obese and coughing and he had discharge coming from one of his eyes. It really sucked; if we'd been able to take him before the one-week waiting period, he would not have been sick. They gave me a ten-day supply of doxycycline and eyedrops and said, "Just keep him away from all other animals."

"Um, what about our dog?" I asked, stupidly.

"You have another dog?" Lisa said, like I'd been trying to hide something.

Paul jumped in. "Yes."

Starting to move on to her next project, she declared, "You need to keep them separated."

"We live in a New York City apartment," I said and held my hands close together to indicate that our apartment was only four inches wide.

She shrugged and said, "Well, your other choice is to leave him here and get him in ten days."

We didn't know what to do. I called Sheryl on my cell phone. I briefed her and she said, "Oh, bloody hell!" Most of us with dogs that aren't boarded opt out of the kennel cough vaccine. I was trying to remember if Bea had had it. I knew she had it when she was young because the breeder had given it to her, but I wasn't sure if that would still be effective.

"Can you call the vet?" Sheryl said. It was Sunday. The vet was upstate, and they weren't open. The thing was, we really wanted to get Sherlock out of there. It wouldn't be good for him to stay there in his condition; clearly, he was not thriving. We decided to take him. Worst case, if Beatrice got the cough, she'd get treated. She was such a healthy dog, so we crossed our fingers and signed Sherlock out.

The first step was putting on the collar we brought for him. It was like trying to harness a whale with a ponytail holder. The collar was the largest one we had—a size medium. Bea wore a petite/extra-small. Sherlock was more of the Big and Tall variety. Fortunately, they sold collars at the shelter and we picked out a lovely teal harness and matching leash that were probably meant for a Newfoundland or a Saint Bernard. The man who worked in the store also gave Sherlock a free stuffed animal—a white squeaky dog and a pink one for Violet.

We planned to walk him a few blocks; we were all the way at the East River Drive and needed to get closer to where we could find a cab. So we started sauntering. Sherlock took about five steps and lay down. Coughing and wheezing, a puma he was not. Paul finally remarked that he had to go to work in less than twenty-four hours, so we needed to move a little quicker . . . than backward. So he picked Sherlock up with an audible groan and carried him, noting that in addition to his health conditions he stank like the monkey house.

So Sherlock the dog sprawled out on the backseat of a cab, and Paul the large man and me the tall woman and Violet the human child squished into the windows first for space and then for air. We dragged him out of the car and insisted he walk the five feet to the apartment building. I went up to the apartment and got Beatrice so the two could meet on equal footing, not on her turf. She wanted to go for an energetic walk and he just wanted to find a place to rest. I ended up walking Bea and Paul took Slim, as we called him, home.

He didn't do much of anything but pant. He found a cool spot of wood floor and lay down (well, more like crumpled). He didn't want much to do with us or anything, and we had no idea, really, what he was like. It was still a "shock" period.

I posted to the group to let them know we had him.

> We picked Sherlock up today from CACC (the NYC pound). He has kennel cough, heavy nasal discharge, and some eye issues (mild nuclear sclerosis, corneal scarring) and a lot of extra weight on him. He looks like he has sway-back and he's got splayed paws. Other than that, he's as

sweet as can be, a gentle and frightened little soul. Between the coughing and the extra weight, it's a little nerve-racking at the moment; he also won't eat anything yet (he's drinking a lot of water). I have a ten-day supply of doxy for him and got the first dose down (not easy since he isn't interested in food). Other than that we're all taking turns lying on the floor with him and talking to him and Violet's singing "Old MacDonald" to him, which he seems to enjoy. I'm holding off on bathing him until he settles down, poor thing! I'll keep you posted!

Julie

Cut to two days later. He didn't get to that size by not being interested in food. We started seeing glimpses of the real Sherlock (Paul was calling him Sherlock Homeless) on day three when I put food down for each dog and he sprinted to his bowl and vaporized it. After licking the bowl clean, he looked up at me; there was a piece of kibble on his nose, but not for long. No food was safe. Getting a little something in his tummy, and a few days of antibiotics under his belt, started bringing him around. He was a fat boy, but he had moves. Well, one move. Humping. He humped Bea. Then he humped the coffee table, his bed (that one made sense to me), and finally, us. I shoved him off, but Violet had more difficulty. I spent my time guarding her from Sherlock's "funny dancing."

By the end of week one, he was spry and spirited. His walking was immeasurably better; i.e., he did it without collapsing. And after a bath and a nail clipping, during which we sang the "Merry Old Land of Oz" makeover music (*Can you even dye my eyes to match my gown? Uh-huh! Jolly old town!*), why, Sherlock was ready for his close-up. If he didn't eat the camera first!

When the antibiotics course was done, Sherlock became his own dog. And he was kind of a pain in the ass. He barked and leaped at Bea and tried to take her on. And, oh, the humping! Though he had fifteen pounds on her, she was the alpha and they started scrapping it up, which we hated. He also started marking his territory—peeing on the edge of the sofa, the bed, my desk. He ripped apart the stuffed animal the shelter gave him and tore the eye off of Violet's before "marking" it as well.

"Why can't he go back to being a blob, Mom?" she asked.

As the second week was nearing, I gave Mary Lou his photos and a biography for her to put on Petfinder and our site so we could start getting some applicants and send him to his "furever" home.

"Has he lost weight?" Sheryl asked me on the phone.

"Ummmmm," I sang, "well, he doesn't look like he's about to explode anymore."

"That's something!" she replied.

I figured he must have been burning a fair amount of calories with his sex simulations.

We knew someone was going to see his photo and fall in love. He was a big fella and that appealed to a lot of people. He kind of reminded me of the cartoon dog Muttley, or an illustration of an English bulldog often seen on New York City T-shirts.

A few days after the ad was placed, a man contacted Sheryl. He wanted Sherlock as a playmate for his Boston terrier. Paul and I were extremely happy; the big fat end was in sight. The man filled out an application, and the people in the group did what they did—interviewed him, called his references and his vet, and arranged a home check. He really wanted Sherlock. It was early in the week and he was willing to drive into Manhattan—seven hours—and pick him up from me on Friday night. The problem was there were no members of the rescue group living close to him, so the home check was really difficult to arrange. Since he'd adopted from a boxer rescue before, I asked Sheryl if we could call them and find out if they'd done a home check. She agreed. We often worked with other rescue groups in that way. I frequently did home checks for groups that didn't have members in New York City. I checked the Boxer Rescue website and our applicant was on there with his dogs in the Success Stories, so that was already good. I left a message for them and e-mailed them to find out what they knew. The woman who had done his home check got in touch and said they had a lovely, well-kept home and were great owners. All was good and I made the arrangements.

Whenever I was fostering I tended to look at the group site less. Sheryl and Joy always included me on their e-mail exchanges, though, since we all could use as many laughs as we could get.

An e-mail went to Joy from Sheryl and I was CC'd. It was a forward:

Joy, would you mind getting back to this person, please?

Sheryl

To Northeast Boston Terrier Rescue:

Today I did a home check through Basset Hound Rescue. There were two Boston terriers there. I brought my very mellow neutered male who usually gets along with everyone. The two Bostons barked/nipped, etc., mainly showing territory. I am wondering if you have any experience with the combinations of basset hounds and Boston terriers and if you think they could get along successfully. In this case, the female Boston was resource guarding around her human. The male did initiate play as we were leaving, but the female interrupted it.

My opinion is it would have to be the right basset and lots of work with the owners to get it set up right.

Thanks for any opinion in this matter.

—Marjorie
"I'd rather be quilting!"

Joy wrote back:

I love you, girlfriend, but why do you send this stuff to me???? I'm going to e-mail her and tell her that Bostons have a genetic predisposition to NOT like bassets—in fact, Bostons consider bassets a rare delicacy to be savored one bite at a time once they are finished screwing them!!!!

Sheryl responded:

Now you see, Julie, why I had to think long and hard about Joy being on the board.

> Joy, I sent it to you because I ran out of steam with all the other crap—and after a glass of wine (or three), I couldn't think of anything smart to say. So, I see that you have. You might add that ears that long are meant to be swung from.

I relished having a part in this club.

But then I got back to my situation. Thursday came and Sherlock and Beatrice got into a real tear-up and though she came away unscathed, his eye was injured and swollen shut. I'd seen that before with Otto many times. It was probably a scratched cornea. I raced him to the vet and got the drops and ointment. I told them he was being adopted the next day and they said it was fine as long as the new owner took him to follow up with their own vet. It was the kind of injury that was fairly common but if untreated could turn serious and lead to the loss of an eye.

I called our man and gave him the choice—I could keep Sherlock until it healed or he could take Sherlock and take it over. He wanted him now. End of story.

It was raining on Friday night, but Sherlock's new dad arrived right on time. He was a burly guy and paid me in cash. He wasn't sure if he was parked legally so he was hurrying, but I made him stop to hear what the eye treatment was. Sherlock and he fell in love immediately, and I was patting myself on the back. I had asked him to keep me posted and he e-mailed me the next morning:

> Hello, Everyone.
>
> What a ride—I was on the road for 7 hours, but it was worth every mile! Julie, you have done a miraculous job!! "Sherlock" is not afraid of or intimidated by anyone or anything. He instinctively knew how to play "Who's your daddy?" and has "Baxter" on the defense (for now).
>
> We absolutely love him. He has the most wonderful disposition. He's going to instantly become the neighborhood favorite tonight at the evening school field "doggie dance nightly gathering." I can tell that this will be a match made in heaven; he and Baxter are starting to chase each other and play. They will wear each other out each day, which was exactly what I was hoping for. They look great together too—a perfect contrast.
>
> We feel so blessed to have him—He is so wonderful—It must have been very difficult for you to part with him. Thanks.

It was my first successful placement, from pulling to homing. And I was feeling quite pleased with myself . . . until Tuesday.

The woman who'd done the home check, the one who said how great a home this guy would be, forwarded me an e-mail from the woman who fostered the boxer he'd adopted from them. It said, "DO NOT LET THIS MAN ADOPT FROM ANYONE! HE KILLED MY DUSTY! I WILL ALWAYS FEEL RESPONSIBLE FOR LETTING HIM HAVE ONE OF MY BABIES!!!"

It was a little loony-sounding, but discomfiting nonetheless. I forwarded it to Sheryl and responded to the woman, saying, based on your recommendation he's got my foster now. What was the story here?

She said the woman heard that he'd let the boxer out in his front yard where there was no fencing even though he'd promised never to do it and the dog had been hit by a car and killed. Now, he'd told us that he had a boxer who died from cancer. None of this was making sense. When we went back to the vet, they said they'd treated a dog for seizures and then put it to sleep on the day after the other dog was killed. They had no record of a dog who'd been hit by a car.

At this point, we were freaking out. Number one, this had all been hidden from us, and number two, it was starting to sound like he had two dogs killed in a two-day period; number three, he had Sherlock. It had also been four days and this vet had not seen Sherlock about his eye and no appointment had been made.

I was totally second-guessing myself, wondering if I had tried to push all of this through because I was anxious for Sherlock to move on. I spoke to Sheryl and she said, "Don't even go there. He was recommended with flying colors and even if someone had visited him, this isn't something we would have known." Either way, I was anxious to get it resolved.

We decided to have Mary Lou call him. If it seemed like he had lied, we should take Sherlock back. There were too many loose ends. I called the Boxer Rescue contact listed on that website and the woman called me back to say her group had split from the one I talked to, and that she knew this guy was on the DNA (do not adopt) list. I suggested she take him off their website success stories.

So Mary Lou called. We were talking about whether to make up a story that some blood test that had been done on Sherlock came back positive and we needed to get him back. And if he said no, should we just steal him?

When Mary Lou called, he told her he'd been expecting to hear from her. For whatever reason, Boxer Rescue was trying to ruin his life. Then he told her the story. The boxer had cancer and had been having seizures. Tragically, he "got out" of the house, wandered into the street, and was hit by a car.

Mary Lou is tough but she's a good and fair judge of character. "I spoke to him for about forty-five minutes," she said, "and one thing that stuck in my head was that Boxer Rescue never would have known what happened to the dog—he reported the accident to them and they freaked out. While none of us likes to see anything happen to our prior fosters, there are a lot of dogs we never hear about again and go on faith that they are fine." She said he didn't seem like a bad guy to her and he did say if we wanted Sherlock back, while it would break his heart, he'd understand. That made all of us feel a lot better. Then he sent me an e-mail:

Julie,

There seems to be some controversy regarding my last pet—Although being hit by a car, the root cause of him uncharacteristically wandering off was the effects of the recently diagnosed brain tumor. I spoke with one of your senior NEBTR volunteers the other day, and fully explained the horrid turn of events. I also reassured her, and wish to reassure you as well, that I am a lifelong dog lover, and treat and have treated all my pets with extreme care and oversight. As I said to her, Send as many home adoption inspectors as you wish, as often as you wish. The forwarded attached message should also help to clear the controversy.

On a good note, Sherlock is very happy, and we love him. He and Baxter are bonding, and it is an absolute joy to witness. They have advanced from the initial humping stage, which had Baxter on the defense, to what I would call the "wet neck" stage. They love to attempt to gnaw on each other's neck, until they drop from exhaustion. Also, I am very happy to report that they have selected one (of many) toys that they love to play "tug of war" with (which I consider a milestone development). Sherlock's right eye is completely healed and looks the same as the left eye. I will take him to my vet on Wednesday for a follow-up appt. I've been trying to capture some "Kodak" moments, but they are too fast for the camera. I will have photos very soon. Please forward this message to the NEBTR lady that I spoke to recently—I did not ask for her e-mail address. Thanks.

ARCHIE THE BOXER'S DEATH [e-mail message that he sent to the woman who approved him]

Although we have never met, I feel a stronger connection to you than anyone else in boxer rescue. Therefore I am responding in general to you, in hopes of appeasing some other volunteers that seem to have categorized me as a heartless murderer of defenseless animals, and wish for my crucifixion. Again, I accept full responsibility for Archie's death, and will be haunted more so than anyone by that guilt forever.

However, am I to be judged on one momentary lapse of judgment, which tragically resulted in the death of my precious loving Archie??!!—We were in love!! Please remind everyone of all the good boxer work that I have done over the years—in particular with Elmore, who no one wanted due to his fear aggression issues.

I adopted him, rehabilitated him, and gave him the best years of his remaining life. I have never discounted the adult/senior adoptable boxers, and have adopted them exclusively knowing full well that my home was their last stop before dog heaven, without regard for end stage life medical expenses, and emotional trauma.

My heart has no more strings to pull, and I agree not to ever again attempt to adopt a boxer (and will be content with two Boston Terriers that have a much longer life expectancy).

In the end we decided to send Joy to do a home check as quickly as possible. If she felt the home was not safe, she would take Sherlock with her. She did it and said that although they were a little wacky, they were good wacky and her recommendation was to leave Sherlock right where he was.

Which we did.

I felt ultimately good about Sherlock's placement, but it made me think a lot about what makes a good home for a pet. A while back there was a discussion in our group about the automatic "no" someone wanted to give to an applicant who was single and worked away from home eleven hours a day. One of the board members, a single working mother, said, "If that's the case, then you wouldn't give me a dog." The person argued that we *know* our board member and what a good dog parent she is. It was a lengthy debate and one that was never quite settled. Look at me, I was single, living in a tiny studio, and working when I got Otto. Could there have been a better home for him out there? I think not!

When you're looking for a home for your foster, you want everything to be perfect. A loving family with a fenced-in yard, who can afford to take care of the sometimes very costly medical issues that come up. The benefit of a whole fenced-in yard is a big issue. I live in an apartment, so my dogs are only walked on leashes, but no matter how careful you are, accidents can happen. Archie's death was an accident, just as Moses's death was. There is so much to consider, but fundamentally you are considering a person who is choosing to adopt from a rescue group, not buying from a pet shop in a mall.

When the story started to unfold, and we thought that we'd been misled, I thought for sure Sherlock was coming back to me. It was totally enlightening to me that Joy and Mary Lou allowed for there to be a gray area. Their collective good judgment and sanity were a relief and for that I was grateful. There have to be strict guidelines in place for potential adopters, and a group has to be allowed to turn people down. Like people who spontaneously buy a $2,000 dalmatian in a pet shop after seeing the Disney movie, then change their minds when they see what having a dalmatian actually means, and drop the dog at the front door of the local animal shelter, not everyone is meant to have a dog. There are times when a dog is placed in the most perfect home, only to be returned to the group because the perfect people were unhappy. That wouldn't make us stop placing dogs in perfect homes, and by the same token taking the time to look a little closer at what might not sound ideal on paper could lead a dog to the happiest place he will ever go.

LESSON NINE

How to Feel Good About Your Neck

By the time I turned forty, Madonna, Sheryl Crow, Michelle Pfeiffer, and Kim Basinger had all *fortied* stunningly. So I didn't have an issue with the age at all. Nothing would be different from thirty-nine. I wasn't going to suddenly start wearing longer skirts or cut my hair above my shoulders. I was still me, though I do remember looking up "middle age" in the *Oxford English Dictionary,* where I was slightly relieved to see it defined as beginning at forty-five. The one good-bye I said was to my future second child. I felt very strongly that my body wouldn't be able to handle a pregnancy after forty (it hadn't done that well at thirty-six). While I saw a multitude of women having first, second, third, and fourth babies after forty, and doing it gracefully, it was just something I didn't feel I could manage. And it was an easy decision, except that it wasn't. Even after I made it, I internally debated it nonstop and occasionally discussed my conclusions with Paul. Was it selfish to have only one child? I adored my brothers. Would I be depriving Violet of something that meant so much to me? But if I did it and was miserable—which I was convinced I would be—wouldn't everyone suffer? And once we had the baby, I wouldn't be able to work; with the kind of money I made, we couldn't afford the amount of child care we'd need. I had finally gotten into this nice rhythm with taking Violet to school, going to the gym, and getting a chunk of work time in before I had to pick her up after school. And I liked being the one to drop her off and pick her up. Everything was just the way I wanted it . . . so I had to punish myself. If it was that good for me, it must be a lousy, selfish act. The one thing I knew was the more time I spent debating it, the less chance there'd be that I'd ever be able to do it. Suffice it to say, I drove a lot of people nuts and carved in some new worry lines in the process.

It was the summer before Violet started kindergarten and we were doing lots of trips instead of camp—to my parents' home on the New York/Vermont border, Mattie's house in Montauk, and to visit my brother Matt in Washington, D.C.

Matt and I talked about the issue of a second child. He and his wife were going through a similar struggle. They had a child and felt like they should have another, but weren't sure it was the right thing.

"Why don't you get a dog?" I asked Matt. My mother and I spent a fair amount of time on the phone talking about how it was possible that Matt, who had been the dog kid in our family, was the only one of us who'd grown up not to have one.

"I can't take the responsibility," he said.

"Of what?"

"Walking it, feeding it," he said, as if he were saying something that was very much harder than walking and feeding.

"You have a yard!" I responded. "Just open the back door and let it out!"

"We don't have the space!" he said.

"How come you live in an entire house with a front yard and a backyard and you don't have space, but I live in an apartment in the city and I do have space?" I wondered aloud.

"Maybe," he said, "if we don't end up having another kid." (Before he'd had his first child, he had told me if that didn't happen, he was going to get a Ferrari.)

Paul had to work, so he stayed back in New York with Bea. We were in a nice single-dog calm. Joy was putting pressure on me to adopt a dog she was fostering. An elderly gentleman by the name of Edgar. He had a medical issue that we were waiting to hear about, but Joy thought he was another Moses. Paul and I talked about it (with about the same ease as the kid issue). He wasn't crazy about the idea; an old dog with health problems sounded like a lot of heartbreak, but I had long wanted to take in a senior. They were the last to be adopted; not many people were looking to get a dog who was in its twilight years. And the old ones always broke my heart. Once we heard what the surgeon said about Edgar, I'd revisit the discussion with Paul.

Two nights before we were due to come back to New York from D.C., Paul called. He said that Jane, the intake coordinator, had left a voicemail and that it was important. I called in and listened to the message myself—a ten-year-old Boston was dumped in the Brooklyn Center for Animal Care and Control (which made the one in Manhattan look like Club Med) by a family who said they could no longer take care of her because of their financial situation. She said she posted on the site and was waiting to hear if anyone could foster her, but in the meantime, could I pull her as soon as possible?

I called Jane back and told her I was coming home from D.C. on Monday and asked if they could hold her until then. She felt like that would be too late and said she'd left a message for a new member in Manhattan to see if he could get her and was waiting to hear back. I told her to call me when she heard. In the meantime, I went on the site.

The post was more personal and urgent than usual:

> There is a ten-year-old female in the Brooklyn shelter that was dumped by her owners because of some problem with their lease. The shelter says she is terrified and won't even hold her head up. The shelter told us that if we want her, we need to get her quickly. We all know what that means. If anyone is available to pull her or more importantly foster this poor old girl so she doesn't die in the shelter please let me know ASAP.

I called her back and said I'd come home a day early. Since I'd still be coming back to Manhattan from D.C., if the other member could get her and let me pick her up from him, that would work better. I could hold her until we found a foster home. The other member agreed.

The next day I came home, kissed Paul hello, dropped Violet off, and jumped on a subway to the West Village to meet this guy. While I waited, I realized it was the exact same block where I'd picked up "Mr. Man/Chip/Shaggy." It must have been some major meeting of doggie gridlines.

A guy was coming down the street with a small black dog

that wasn't a Boston. I didn't remember reading that she was a mix, but clearly this dog was. She didn't have a flat nose or any white markings and she had a long tail. She looked sort of Chihuahua-ish. Maybe this wasn't the dog I was meeting. When the guy got closer he said, "Julie?"

He said her name was Precious and I recoiled. The very fact that a family would dump a dog they called Precious creeped me out. Then I wondered if she was named Precious because of her resemblance to Gollum from *The Lord of the Rings*. Either way, she didn't respond to it so I wasn't going to use it. I took her into a cab. She was so profoundly unresponsive that I wondered if she was dying.

When I got her home, I saw that Paul had placed a dog bed in the living room so she could have her own space away from Bea. Of course Bea had to keep sitting in that bed, and anywhere Precious wanted to go Bea needed to be, really, really badly. Violet was asleep and Paul and I were looking at her. Ten was conservative; I would have put her closer to twelve. She was old, and she was a mess.

"What do you think she is?" he asked.

"Maybe Boston and Chihuahua?" I guessed. She had Boston eyes and ears but a longish nose, no white markings, and a long tail. She would not look at us.

Her muzzle was gray, and it looked like she had at least

the beginnings of cataracts. There were age warts in her fur, fatty masses, bald spots along her tail and behind her ears, and her teeth were rotten. I offered her food and she ignored it. She had some water and once we moved Bea she took over the bed. With her head down, she breathed in a way that sounded like a sigh, and went to sleep.

Paul and I were sitting at our dining-room table looking over at her and discussing the highlights of the weekend. Every so often one of us would say, "Well, she's really no trouble," and "We could foster her for a little while."

The next day I made an appointment with a vet to get her teeth cleaned. The report from the shelter said, "Unable to locate spay scar and *very bad teeth*." They had let her come to rescue without spaying her because she was so old. I posted her photo on the site with a short description and got loads of responses; everybody was just so glad to hear she'd been saved.

In the morning, Violet woke up and met her and asked what her name was.

"You can name her," I said.

"What are some flower names?" she asked.

"Well, Blossom, Iris, Daisy, Rose, Wisteria, Bluebell," I said.

"Bluebell!" she repeated.

"That's nice," I said. "Or Dahlia."

"What does a dahlia look like?" she asked. And we Googled a picture.

"Okay," she asserted, "Dahlia."

Paul called her Black Dahlia after the gruesomely murdered Los Angeles call girl. Apparently her teeth were nasty, too.

We took her to the vet, a new vet. I was at the point where I'd been to just about every vet on the Upper West Side and I had a reason to dislike each of them. This was one I'd gone to with Otto years before, but had stopped because every time I went back, the vet who'd seen him before was gone and replaced with a new one who'd also soon be gone. But I had taken Sherlock there for his eye and I really liked the guy who examined him.

Unfortunately, even though it was only a month later, he was gone, too. So they gave me to the newest victim: a young, enthusiastic vet named Dr. No.

I didn't have a huge amount of faith in her, but she seemed very willing to bring other vets in to look at whatever she wasn't sure of. That was good enough for me. I'd had a similar experience with a pediatrician. I didn't mind a doctor who wasn't the slickest diagnostician as long as he or she utilized other doctors who were.

We talked about the spay issue. She went with the

Brooklyn shelter's "cannot locate spay scar," and talked to me about having her spayed. She told me that although Dahlia wouldn't be able to get pregnant at her age, for health reasons it would be a good idea to spay her. I told her I'd talk to my rescue board about it. It was very costly and possibly dangerous. In the meantime I wanted to get her teeth cleaned. For that she needed to take a series of blood tests to make sure it was safe to put her under anesthesia. She did them and the next day called and said she forgot one and to bring her back; they wouldn't charge me for another office visit.

I wasn't surprised. This was what I'd come to expect from veterinarians in New York City. They all charge a fortune and appear to enjoy every opportunity to do more for more money. They surpass the human doctors I use in expense, except they don't have the continued training that human doctors have, so they're frequently testing unnecessarily or just wildly guessing wrong. A vet's misdiagnosis killed one of my dogs, and though I know and love many vets who've saved dogs, none of them has ever saved me any money. When Beatrice needs shots, I take her to my parents' vet in the country. Office visits in Manhattan range from $60 to $90 for just walking in the door. At my parents' vet, an office visit is $13, and last time I went, they said Bea was so small they only charged me $7.50. Imagine that! Mind you, before I take any of my fosters to the vet, I present them with a letter from Northeast Boston Terrier Rescue that goes something like this:

> We would be most grateful for your consideration to offer a rescue discount on procedures needed for our rescued Boston Terriers, in particular Dahlia, who is being fostered by our volunteer Julie Klam.
>
> It is with generosity like yours that we are able to continue helping the rehabilitation of the body and soul of so many dogs in need.
>
> We understand and agree that this offer is for our foster dogs, and not our personal dogs.
>
> Your bills, which will be paid promptly, can be mailed to the following. Or, if you prefer to have our bank card number, please call the above number. In this case, we would request that an invoice for full services be mailed to the above address.
>
> Thank you for your consideration.

I've brought this letter to several vets for several dogs and not a single one has actually given consideration.

For just the blood tests, the cost is close to $400 and we were not even done with those yet. One more. But no charge for the office visit because she'd forgotten it. What a sport!

I shuttled Dahlia back and forth. She remained in her

dejected state. In other news, Violet's kindergarten was about to begin and the new principal had instituted a mandatory uniform policy, even though it was a public school. Violet had to wear a light blue shirt and a navy blue jumper or long skirt. My daughter would only wear pink and purple, and this, she pointed out to me, was blue and blue. "Boys' colors!" she complained. I was thinking of writing to the governor for a reprieve.

When Dahlia's blood work came back, something wasn't right. Liver functions were off, and there was some blah blah about enzymes. The vet asked for urine so she could further test. I got the urine and dropped it off, and it was still not conclusive, but she had an idea of what it could be. She told me to watch and see if Dahlia's belly looked bloated, or if she was eating more or peeing more. I told her I'd watch and asked her what she thought it was. "Cushing's disease," she said. She listed the symptoms, which included the bald spots and the fatty growths, and said it was something that frequently occurred in older dogs. It seemed pretty likely. The vet just needed me to get the first urine of the day. Well, that would be tough, I said, since lately the first urine of the day was on my carpet.

"Okay," she said, "just do the best you can."

I looked up Cushing's disease and found out that it has to do with the pituitary gland malfunctioning, creating an excess of blood cortisol. In effect, the dog is being poisoned with too much cortisol and cannot rely on its own feedback mechanism to regulate the blood cortisol level. The good news was that it was treatable; the bad but somehow very unsurprising news was that the medication was extremely costly. Big shockaroo.

So I had my miserable daughter who hated her uniform, as well as her new glasses and her new school, and my old foster who now most likely had a disease with a fancy name. She would sneak-pee outside, camouflaging her moves so I wouldn't know she was peeing until after the puddle was there and my would-be sample went running down the sidewalk. Occasionally she peed in a sitting position, so as soon as she started to sit I jammed the cup under her. Nada. Sometimes I got lucky enough to get some pee on my hand.

I felt very sorry for Dahlia, but I wasn't in love with her. But someone else in the family was. Violet would sit by Dahlia in her bed, set up tea parties for the two of them, and sing long, made-up songs about Queen Dahlia and the magical fairies of the enchanted wood. She read Dahlia books and selected videos for Dahlia to watch. Paul and I looked on, trying to figure it out. Dahlia was the least charismatic animal either of us had ever come across and yet Violet saw her as the belle of the ball.

My concern was that because of her age and her looks, no

one was going to see her photo on Petfinder and say, "I want that warty, bald, cateracty, fatty-tumorous canine of indeterminate breed, pronto!" She just wasn't a cover girl, except maybe for *Modern Maturity*'s dog edition. I put on my Francesco Scavullo hat and started snapping pictures of her. She was pretty much always in that bed, so I moved it around to get different backgrounds and improved lighting. One of her messed-up teeth sort of hung out of the side of her mouth, so I tried to get her to look the other way. After two hours and twenty pictures where she looked exactly the same with not much behind the eyes, I quit. I e-mailed the best ones and wrote what I hoped was an emotional plea to a potential adopter.

> Dahlia, a beautiful BT mix, is by far the sweetest dog any of us has ever met. When she should have been gently sailing into her sunset years, she was cruelly dumped into a miserable city animal shelter for no reason at all. Dahlia is in terrific shape at the age of nine with many good years ahead of her. On a walk, she is curious and attentive. She's great on a leash and housebroken. In a home, she is respectful and peaceful. She is wonderful with all dogs, big and small, as well as children young and old. She loves to cuddle and kiss and is heartbreakingly good. She is just looking for someone to love her.

Somewhere we know there is a kind forever family waiting for Dahlia.

I shaved her age a little, just because we really didn't know. And everyone judged her age by her teeth, which were totally rotten. When I got Otto, they told me he was a year and a half old. The first vet I took him to said he was four years old. It was a guess, and I just wanted the guess to be on the younger end so she would have a chance.

After I sent the Petfinder ad, I sat with Dahlia. I had no idea what her life had been like; we knew she'd had multiple litters, but beyond that, not much. She had belonged to someone who felt it was acceptable to put her in a shelter where they had been told she would be killed. My guess was that her life had been hard. I started thinking about her age and her looks and how that would be held against her. When I walked her no one ever stopped to pet her. She had the invisibility of an aging woman with a bad self-image.

There was something about her expression, her eyes, that reminded me of *Migrant Mother*, Dorothea Lange's famous portrait of a farm laborer in the dust bowl of the Depression. The woman, Florence Owens Thompson, was thirty-two in the picture, but she looked to be in her mid-fifties. Maybe Dahlia was younger than she looked; maybe she'd been beaten down by life, too.

Remarkably, we got responses to the Petfinder ad. It was illuminating for me to learn that just as I'd been looking on the site years before for a dog who resembled bulgy-walleyed Otto, there were people out there looking for a dog like Dahlia, too.

And sure enough, the woman who absolutely wanted to have her most of all was someone who'd owned and lost a dog who looked just like her. Her dog, Moonlight, lived to be seventeen. She had gotten her from a neighbor whose dog had puppies right before her husband went overseas during World War II. Moonlight was a mix, also. As for the woman, she was a retired schoolteacher who lived in a small town in upstate New York in a house with a fenced-in yard. She really wanted to meet Moonlight II.

I was utterly charmed by the letter, but I always worried about someone who saw a dog as the return of their long-lost friend. It wasn't that I didn't believe it could happen. I just didn't want her to get Dahlia, find out she wasn't Moonlight, be disappointed, and send her packing again. That was not the reason we didn't let her adopt Dahlia. The reason was when I told Violet, she got terribly upset. She said we couldn't give Dahlia away. Dahlia was her sister! I had really never seen her so emphatic, and she was having such a hard time with school that I thought maybe Dahlia was serving some emotional purpose for her. I was certainly willing to hold off.

We tried to broach the subject with her and frame it in a way that would make her feel comfortable or at least willing to let Dahlia go.

"There is a lonely lady who has no dog to love her and she saw Dahlia's picture and she thinks Dahlia would be the best dog for her."

"Tell her to get her own dog."

"Violet, someone called today and said they have a big yard and a shady tree perfect for Dahlia to lie under."

"Dahlia likes her bed."

"If Dahlia goes to her new home, we will have room to take a new foster, maybe a puppy, maybe we could keep it."

"I don't want a puppy, I want Dahlia."

And so we let it go for a while. At night after she went to bed, we talked about how Violet had become a tireless advocate for this homeless wretch. Was there something this child was seeing that wasn't apparent to us?

She was really unhappy in her school. It was just a bad fit, and I was inexorably pursuing possible alternatives. The other choices were Gifted and Talented for first grade or one of the coveted but filled-to-capacity schools in our district. We'd been in the lottery and didn't get in anywhere. Now the only chance to switch was if a kid moved and a spot opened up. Since there wasn't a waiting list, I just called all of the principals all of the time.

Walking home from school on a Thursday, I told Violet that I had to go to a meeting that night and she'd be having a babysitter. She was exhausted and frustrated and started really crying. I had a hard time responding to her because I agreed with everything she felt. I didn't want to tell her I was trying to find her a new school, in case it didn't happen. I thought we needed a nice distraction. So I told her that if she really wanted to, we would keep Dahlia. While she was jumping up and down and cheering I was kicking myself. How could I have said that without talking to Paul? How could I have said that without thinking of my own feelings? The best we could say was Dahlia was almost no trouble. Pretty much 24/7, she lay in her bed. Though she had come around some, and there were times she even wagged her tail (when Violet came home), she was still kind of a nothing.

I told Paul it reminded me of when I was a kid growing up and a friend of mine had a grandmother who lived with her family. She didn't talk much, or wear flashy jewelry, or have her hair done, or smell good, like my grandmother; she just sat in a chair with her silver bed hair and a frayed men's cardigan, just watching us, and every so often saying, "You shouldn't play so close to the tree," or "Watch it by the pachysandra," or "I don't think your mother wants you running in the house." It was always kind of a bummer when you went there and realized she was out of her room. That was Dahlia to me, the unwanted, kvetchy grandmother.

Paul fake-cried when I told him what I'd done. He said maybe we could trick Violet into changing her mind. Say we found her owner like "Mr. Man/Chip/Shaggy." I said that while I found it admirable that he was working so hard to find a way to cheat our daughter out of her beloved pet, I didn't think we could go back on my word. I got a lot of squinty evil eyes from him, kind of a "just you wait" thing. But I told him if he'd been in the same position that I was, he'd have done the same thing. He said no, it never would have occurred to him. "Couldn't you have gotten her an ice cream or cupcakes?"

I got a call out of the blue that the most desirable of the public schools I'd been nudging might have an upcoming opening. Something was afoot and I could be getting a call any day now. I was elated. This thing that I'd been worrying myself into knots about night and day might magically turn out okay. Sure enough, it did. A spot opened up and we just had to wait until the end of the month for Violet to start.

So I went back to my other work that wasn't my job: trying to get a urine sample from Queen Dahlia.

It was a Friday morning, and I dropped Violet at school. I took the dogs with me so I could walk and drop all in one shot. I was on my cell phone with my mother waiting for Dahlia to pee, and when she went it was like two drips. So I took the dogs home and tried again around noon; this time when she squatted, a gelatinous substance came out. I called the vet while we were walking and I said, "It looks like mucus."

And she said, "Sounds like a urinary tract infection. If it doesn't clear up in the next couple of days, bring her in."

And I hung up and thought, Sure, I'll drop another three hundred bucks to hear "inconclusive."

That weekend we talked up the new school with Violet and went shopping for non-uniform clothes she could wear. We were focused on that change coming in Violet's life, and once I saw that Dahlia was peeing normally, I figured I'd go back to trying to trap it on Monday. Truthfully, we weren't paying that much attention to her. So on Sunday when Dahlia was acting totally crazy, I still didn't think much about it, though I noticed she was eating bathroom garbage and flipping her bed all over the living room. She turned it upside down and around and dragged it into different places and finally put it back where it was, facing the wall instead of the TV. I watched her with my eyebrows wrinkled, thinking, and finally I realized. She was preparing to die. She was very disconnected from us in general, but now it was even more evident. She seemed okay to me, but I didn't hold out hope that she'd make it through the week. A couple of times she got very anxious and agitated, furiously barking at nothing, and I wondered if the Grim Reaper was by her bed. We had Violet stay away from her and told her to skip the good night kiss, so she blew a kiss to her from across the room. Then we read and all went to sleep.

At about four in the morning I woke up in sort of a half-dream state. I had a very strong feeling that Dahlia had passed over. I didn't get up, I just waited. About a half hour later I went to the bathroom and looked out. Dahlia was in her bed, alive. So much for my psychic sense. I went back to sleep, and at 5:30 I was up again. This time I went to the living room. I was really sleepy, my eyes were not all the way open, and I went to the kitchen first to get a drink of water. When I turned on the light I saw Dahlia had had a bad case of diarrhea on the floor. I started unrolling paper towels and heard what sounded like a squeak from the living room. I kept cleaning, and then I heard something else, so I just peeked out to see what was going on. There, inside Dahlia's bed, were some kind of creatures. My first unconscious thought was that they were mice, and then I realized they were black and white and they were puppies. I stood looking at her in shock, like she would turn to me and explain. Dahlia was very peaceful and the puppies were nursing. I ran into the bedroom and said pretty loudly, "Paul, wake up. Dahlia had puppies!" And my husband, who moves especially slowly in the morning, was up like a shot and Violet was right behind him. We all stood around blinking our eyes like it was a crazy dream. Dahlia had been pregnant when we got her from the shelter! All that had been happening with her had to do with the fact that she was getting ready to give birth! It was nothing short of miraculous.

The first thing I whispered to Paul was, "Check and make sure they're not dead."

He went over and looked. There were only two. One was all black and one was black and white like a Boston terrier. And they were both very much alive.

We all sat and looked at them and kept repeating, "I can't believe it." Dahlia was like a seventy-two-year-old woman. My first thought was that I was right about the vet; she was a moron. I was anxious to call Sheryl and find out what I was supposed to do. It was immediately evident that Dahlia was a pro. She had given birth and cleaned up everything while we all slept. She knew she wanted to do this alone, and she did. It explained why she was going so nuts with the bed; she was trying to "nest."

I waited until 7:30 to call my parents' house, where Mattie was visiting. There were several rounds of exclamations of disbelief. After I took Violet to school, I called Sheryl at her home upstate. She didn't answer, and I didn't leave a message, but she saw the caller ID and about one minute later she phoned me back.

"Sheryl? I have some news."

"Oh? Yes?"

"Dahlia didn't have Cushing's disease."

"Oh, great!"

"She had puppies."

(*Pause.*) "I'm sorry?"

I repeated the shocking revelation and we both laughed and laughed. It was the last thing we expected from this old girl.

She did this thing, something so incredibly rare: giving birth as a senior. It made me think about my own misgivings about having a child over forty, and the fearlessness with which Dahlia moved. And what about Violet? Had she known? I had to think she must have had a sense—perhaps Dahlia had communicated it to her—because if it wasn't for Violet, this event would have taken place elsewhere. It was all sorts of amazing. I had a real "right on!" feeling about Dahlia. I had jump-started my career later in life, and I'd been completely astonished by the turns my own life took. When I told various women what had happened, they all gasped and laughed. We were all happy to know that life could surprise us just when we thought we were done.

LESSON TEN

How to Find Happiness

Shock was all we felt. That first day we could not stop repeating, "I can't believe Dahlia had puppies!" "Can you believe Dahlia had puppies?" "How is it possible that Dahlia had puppies?" She did it all herself and cleaned up everything. Ev-ery-thing. And with that Dahlia went from the old annoying grandmother to Eleanor Roosevelt in my eyes.

According to Sheryl, there were a couple of things we needed to do for her. First, make a whelping box (a clean, safe, secluded space for her to take care of her puppies) and then make sure she was assuming her role okay. I learned that a mother of pups needs to nurse and clean up after them and lick their privates to stimulate their ability to go to the bathroom on their own.

I went to the UPS store near my home on Broadway and asked for the largest box they had, which was a square moving box. (I was tempted to get the guitar box so that Dahlia could have a hipper, more modern home.) I followed the directions for putting it together slowly, thinking as I went, How many Jews does it take to make a box? It turned out that it took just one a ridiculously long time. I generously patted myself on the back for being able to do it all by myself. For a doorway, I cut a U shape several inches off the ground so when the puppies were mobile, they wouldn't be able to make the Great Escape. The bottom was lined with multiple layers of the *New York Times*, and on top of that was a baby comforter, and then plush bath sheets that I could easily take out and wash. Across the top, I laid one of Violet's old crib sheets for a canopy, so the dogs would feel cloistered and out of harm's way. I also imagined that they would like the subtle darkness, being ever so slightly removed from the window's light.

All of this was per Sheryl's instructions. She also told me to look under the puppies to see what sex they were. Up until that moment, I didn't want to pick them up. I had thought it was like with baby birds: if I handled them too much, the mother would lose interest in them. But when I moved Dahlia to her stylish new digs, I had to move the babies, too, so I looked then. Not quite as easy as it is with human babies; both dogs had "something" down there. Sheryl told me the girl would look like she had a walnut and the boy, well, a tiny peepee.

I set the whole thing up in Violet's room, since it was out of the way of most of our household traffic. It was about fifty feet from the old bed to the new one, and I walked them like I was going down the aisle. Using my untrained eye, I deduced that the slightly bigger one that was all black was a female, and the smaller, black-and-white one was a male. Though I wouldn't have put money on it. The next day Sheryl came to visit and brought me an X-pen, a metal gate to go around the whole whelping box to give extra safety and room for Dahlia to leave, along with a piece of faux sheepskin. She said when they got a little older it would be better for them to be on that because when they wet it, it would be absorbed. We set up the area and piled newspapers inside the pen for Dahlia. She absolutely refused to leave them the first two days. Sheryl double-checked my work and confirmed my exam. She also said that their noses were very long—not flat like Bostons'—and their ears were huge.

"Well," I said, slightly defensively, "I'm assuming the puppies will grow and their ears will look normal."

She looked over her glasses at me and said emphatically, "They will never, ever grow into those ears."

Along with another member of the rescue, Sheryl was a breeder. She and Victoria shared ownership of a handful of beautiful dogs, which they occasionally bred and frequently showed (and won!). I was so grateful for her expertise; it reminded me very much of Violet's first appointment with the pediatrician. You just want someone who knows something to say, "Yes, you've done well. It's all right."

When she picked up the puppies, I was reminded of when we took eleven-day-old Violet to visit our Lamaze teacher, and we thought she was "throwing" Violet too much. We handled our baby like a handblown glass starfish. While Sheryl checked the puppies' mouths for cleft palate and did a cursory check of their bodies, Dahlia was up at attention, her nose close to them. When Sheryl put them back in with her, Dahlia picked them up and put them behind her and turned her back to us. She gave us one sidelong glance as if to say, "You are done here."

Sheryl also checked Dahlia's teats. She was a little troubled by the lack of milk. Usually when you touched a nursing bitch, milk squirted out. She really had to squeeze to see Dahlia's milk.

"You're going to have to watch that," she said. "If it doesn't come in better, you may have to supplement."

Suddenly I was a mother with a newborn again—two of them, covered in fur. I had read online that for the first six weeks the mother would take care of everything, and only after that would you need to jump in. Now that Sheryl had explained things, it didn't seem like that was the case. The other thing she mentioned was that, really, the puppies were quite vulnerable and while they looked well, if something happened they could easily pass away.

"When are they considered 'out of the woods'?" I asked.

"Four to six weeks," she said, "though I've known people to lose puppies at nine weeks." She wasn't trying to worry me. She just wanted me to realize this wasn't over yet, not by a long shot. I would need a small scale to weigh them daily, and if they weren't gaining weight or, worse, were losing it, I'd have to supplement them with puppy formula.

Weighing them was the only time I touched them at first. Their eyes were still closed and they were so dependent on their mother that it was rattling to take them from her, for me and for the puppies. Unsurprisingly, they didn't just sit in the pan on the scale and wait. Looking more like hamsters than puppies, they tried to get their little bodies out of there. I had considerable difficulty getting an accurate number, but I did my best and I then dutifully recorded what I saw in a composition notebook.

I didn't want Dahlia to fret, so I tended to do the weighing as quickly as I could. She was the very picture of a natural mother, and she was so incredibly protective of her pups that

I wondered if her earlier litters had been taken from her too quickly. Where had her older children gone?

I lay on the floor with my face at the whelping box and watched her nurse, lick, and nuzzle the pups. I decided at that moment that Dahlia would never leave us. As long as it was in my power, she'd never be afraid or wonder where her home was again, and I told her so. I found myself loving her so much, I could barely stand it. She was like a refugee. Dumped in that shelter, examined, caged, picked up, brought to my house. No one had known what she knew, that she was pregnant.

I cooked for her three times a day: chicken or cheeseburgers mixed with puppy food, and cottage cheese and yogurt for snacks. She needed as much as anything to be nourished, which we would have been doing before she gave birth had we known what was about to happen. I brought her meals to her bed, and she leaned her head over and gobbled them up. Some other people in my house wondered if I'd ever cook for them again. "Of course," I said, "just as soon as you have your puppies."

But I worried. As hard as she tried, she was still the equivalent of a seventy-two-year-old woman. Her milk wasn't coming in that fully yet and it might never. Just as I did when Violet was a newborn, I worried that the babies were being starved and that they might die from it. I spoke to Sheryl several times a day, and by day three, I was full-on flipping out. It seemed as though they'd lost weight. We were dealing in minuscule amounts with fidgety puppies, but I felt pretty sure their weight had gone down and I panicked. And I worried about dehydration. Sheryl had said there was a test you could do by pulling the puppies' fur. If they were hydrated it would go back, but if they were dehydrated it would stay. I did this and stared at the fur. I couldn't tell for sure, but my sense was that they were seconds from death. It was late on a Friday, and I called Sheryl on my cell as I walked to the pet store. She told me to get the puppy formula Esbilac, eyedroppers, and tiny doll bottles. I picked them up at a large chain pet store, and while the cashier was looking for the prices, I stepped over to the ID machine and made an engraved tag—a red heart that said "Dahlia Klam-Leo" with our phone number.

I brought home the supplies and started sterilizing and heating the milk—just as I'd done with Violet, testing it on my forearm to make sure it was not too hot, not too cold. The formula smelled and looked like baby formula, so it was flash-back hell. I tried the bottles first with no luck. The puppies couldn't suck yet, so I went to the eyedropper. I also burped them in between feedings. They coughed, since they were not really experts in swallowing yet. Sometimes they'd just let the milk sit in their teeny mousy mouths. Paul came home from work and found me feeding them with my face all pinched in worry.

"I am definitely, *definitely* not having another kid!" I said.

We took turns supplementing them, and I got up to feed them once every night. They were still nursing, and they always fell asleep after eating so most of the time it seemed like they were getting enough from Dahlia, but sometimes I just had the feeling that they were still hungry. The next day I noticed they'd stayed the same weight, and I called Sheryl to see what to do next. She e-mailed her breeder friends to ask if any of them had experience with a senior nursing bitch. (I have never gotten used to that use of the word "bitch.") No one did. It seemed no one anywhere had. I Googled every combination of words—"Senior Bitch," "Nursing," "Giving Birth," "Senior Mother," "Old dog babies"—to try to find someone who'd dealt with this issue before and was totally unsuccessful. Then Sheryl had a thought. The breeder I got Beatrice from had been Otto's veterinarian and then retired. He was well-known in the Boston terrier world. She called him for me and found that he'd actually left retirement and gone back to work, but he was an observant Jew and it was Yom Kippur, so he was unavailable. He did give her instructions for me, though, which were to feed the pups 50 milliliters *every two hours*. Every two hours. Day and night. I started to get weepy. I was already exhausted from this and the idea of waking myself up every two hours during the night was pushing me over the edge. Here I had decided not to have another baby, and yet I was being called upon to be a night nurse! I loved these puppies and I did not want them to die, especially for Dahlia's sake, but I also knew that if I had to spend the next several weeks doing round-the-clock puppy feedings, I wasn't going to make it. I tried not to get ahead of myself. I just set out to do the one night, and I did. Like I had with my own baby, I ended up staying awake the whole night. It was so similar to that experience, the dim lights in the baby's room, the small, hushed movements, scanning out the city windows for a trace of someone being awake. . . . It was lovely until the point when I started thinking about getting Violet to school in the morning and then going to a meeting. How on earth would I do it? Was there a puppy nurse I could hire to do nights?

The next day I said flat out to Sheryl that I wasn't going to be able to manage this myself. We had to figure something out. She decided to call one of the big breeders she knew to see if they had a litter and if we could put our puppies in with them. The problem was, they were seven hours away, but even worse, it would mean we'd have to separate them from Dahlia. When Violet was born, she went right into neonatal intensive care while I was in recovery, and the experience of not being able to see her for almost twenty hours was a much greater hell than the eighteen-hour labor. She in her bassinet and me in my hospital bed both hooked up to machines and wires that made it impossible to move. I didn't think I could willingly do that to Dahlia.

The vet said we could bring her in with the puppies and he would see how everyone was doing. I took a small Fresh Direct box and, except for the door, replicated the whelping box, complete with one of their baby blankets. I placed the puppies inside, and then I put Dahlia's halter and leash on. She was going nuts, jumping up to the box. She weighed twenty-five pounds before she was nursing, so there was no way I was going to carry her and the puppies. When we got in the elevator, I put the box down to adjust my jacket and Dahlia hopped in with them. In fact, I was going to carry her and the puppies. Her butt didn't fit in the box but she was happily nuzzling her pups. I was so filled with empathy for her. I would've jumped in the box with Violet, too.

When we got to the vet, he checked them for dehydration. They were fine, and I saw that the fur wasn't supposed to "snap back" like a slingshot as I had pictured. He also said that Dahlia had *some* milk, and he felt that given her improved diet with lots of calcium, it would come in even more, especially if the puppies continued to nurse. I was told to bring her back in three days and he would check her again.

At that point, he would consider giving her something to boost her milk production, but only if it was needed. Every choice was more difficult to make because of her age. It was very different from treating a young mother dog. Now that it seemed like there was some end in sight, I agreed to keep up the night feedings. In a few days her milk did come in (*hurray!*) and I was able to stop.

I related to Dahlia so much during this time it was freaky. She would sometimes leave the whelping box and come into the living room and get in her former bed. It was like you could hear her saying, "I need a break! When is it going to be time for me?" She'd sit out there for fifteen minutes, her paw covering her eyes with her imaginary cup of General Foods International Coffee, a bathtub filled with Calgon, and then go back for more. Whenever she left the puppies for a break or a walk, she'd wrap them up in the blanket, partly for warmth and partly to keep them out of the sight of any predators.

There was something so extraordinary about seeing true animal instincts up close. In your average household dog, you may see squirrel chasing or some deep sniffing of a dead rodent or the psychotic burying of a bone that reminds you, "Oh right, this is an animal." But Dahlia's mothering seemed so far advanced from that, or maybe it was just that I'd never seen it. Beatrice, who before the birth was totally dominant over Dahlia, would walk great wide circles to avoid going anywhere near the puppies. Even her instincts were heightened.

When I talked to another group member about the milk issue, she told me the story of how a spayed female poodle had been able to create milk and nurse kittens! I looked at Beatrice, who was comfortably resting on the bed. If she'd been a person she would have been looking at her nails and yawning. "I don't think Bea's going to be lactating anytime soon."

At that point, we started to discuss the future. Paul wanted to keep the male. He was so outnumbered by females in our household, and I agreed. The idea of keeping a puppy was kind of exciting. We told Violet she could name them both, but made it clear we were only going to keep the male.

We talked while walking home from the playground and stopped at a cart for a rainbow ice.

"I don't want the boy!" she wailed. "I want the girl!"

I shrugged and repeated her teacher Ms. Davis's saying, "You get what you get and you don't get upset."

Somehow it worked.

"And," I added, "you can name them both. They're both going to be with us for two months, so she'll need a name as well."

"What are some names?" she asked me. And I started

going through all of our rejected baby names: "Francesca, Gianni, Ellis . . ."

She was thinking, her mouth rimmed with glistening red and blue. "I want them to have flower names, like Dahlia."

I rattled off the common flower names and the more unusual ones. At the time, Violet was heavily into the My Little Pony franchise and her favorite girly horse was named Wisteria. I reminded her of that and she jumped on it. "Yes! Wisteria."

If we'd been keeping the girl, I never would've suggested it. No one was going to want to yell, *Wisteria!* It was a big, odd mouthful. Four syllables on this little tiny puppy!

She then moved on to the boy. "What are boy flower names?" she asked. I couldn't think of any—though I thought Briar might work; it was masculine and prickly.

"Brian!" She laughed. "We can't name him Brian!" That was my brother's name.

"Bri-ER," I said. She wasn't interested.

"Or," I said, "we could name him Fiorello. Fiorello means 'little flower' in Italian. There was a mayor named Fiorello LaGuardia who everyone loved." We thought Daddy, with his Italian heritage, would like that one, too.

"Fiorello," she repeated. "Okay, Fiorello and Wisteria."

Things were starting to feel less crazy and more fun.

When we told people the story of Dahlia and the puppies, we'd get the same stunned response followed by, *"How did you not know she was pregnant?"*

It made sense to me that we hadn't known. Her symptoms were the same as Cushing's disease. Paul said that one night he was walking her and an old woman said to him, "Her tits are bigger than mine!" Again, we figured they were just exceedingly hangy because she'd had a lot of litters and she was old. She probably hadn't had postbaby exercise classes to get her figure back. Everything in hindsight sounded stupid. I ended up feeling like one of those girls who live in the backwoods of nowhere who has a baby in the bathroom during a school dance and then goes on *Maury Povich* to talk about it. "I looked in the toilet and there it was!"

The other question people asked after hearing the story was, "Do you know who the father is?"

Do we know who the father is? She was dumped, pregnant, in a shelter in East New York, Brooklyn. Unfortunately, he never called or wrote or sent flowers. Paul said whoever he was, he must have had his beer goggles on that night. Poor Black Dahlia.

"Yeah, but who do you *think* the father was?" they'd press.

"Um, Brad Pitt?"

They wanted answers. They wanted to know what kind

of dog the father was. Well, what kind did we *think* he was? *What kind of dogs are they?*

"Holsteins."

MORE AND MORE BEATRICE was trying to reassert her role. One morning she was bustling with curiosity and went too close to the whelping box. Dahlia growled and Bea growled back and they got into a nasty scuffle. Beatrice was bleeding around the neck, but after it was cleaned up she was fine. Dahlia was squinting. Her left eye had been hurt. I was about to go to Miami for work for two days (everything always happened this way) and I raced her to the vet. After checking her eye, he said she had a deep scratch and uveitis, a condition where part of the uvea, the part of the eye that supplies blood to the retina, becomes inflamed. The inflammation causes proteins to leak out, resulting in cloudiness in the eye. If left untreated, Dahlia could lose her eye. She needed topical drops and antibiotics, which meant we would need to stop her from nursing the puppies and we'd have to go back to feeding them again. So, sorry, the vet said, she just can't nurse. My first thought was, How the hell are we going to keep them from nursing? Separate her from her puppies? AY! And then my mind flashed to Paul, who would be taking care of Violet and Dahlia and Beatrice and the two puppies for two days. Various unpleasant visuals passed through my brain, all of them ending in a very large, angry Paul head. "No," I said. Just flat-out no. *There had to be another option.* The vet said he could call a specialist to see if she could come up with an alternative. He called a doctor friend and explained the situation. He said I had two small children, and I decided not to contradict that. What if it was that extra kid that made my situation sound that much more dire? Violet was easy, but our little lame Tiny Tim, with the tubercular cough, well, that was just too much for any dad.

I took Dahlia to the emergency specialist and forked over a lot of dough, but it was worth anything—*anything*—because she said (1) she just needed eyedrops, and (2) she would still be able to nurse. I told the emergency vet that I loved her and she was the new beneficiary in my will.

The eye healed, and the puppies grew. And watching them develop was breathtaking. Human children's changes are remarkable, but animals grow up so much faster. From bumbling blindly around the box with their little fat bodies bumping into things and then, slowly, opening their eyes. We picked them up more and more, socializing them with kisses and receiving immeasurable joy from them. Countless times I found myself walking around the house thinking, Happiness really *is* a warm puppy!

PAUL, WHO WASN'T QUITE as earnest, kept reenacting the scene from *Apocalypse Now* where they find the puppy in the barrel on the boat. *"Look what she was hiding. See what she was running for. A fucking puppy."*

OUR NEXT-DOOR NEIGHBORS, John and Elisabeth, were pretty serious dog people. They became like the godparents, frequently stopping by for a little "puppy time." Our apartments had back doors from the kitchens into a common hallway, and often when I'd open the door to take out the trash, their door would whip open. "Oh, hey, can we see the puppies?" or "We're having a dinner party. Is it okay if we show everyone the puppies?" It was so charming and fun even if their guests, who were not necessarily dog people, were not quite as engaged as John and Elisabeth.

The puppies weren't going outside yet. In New York City, puppies have to have all of their inoculations before they can go out on the street with other dogs. So they just stayed in the box, and they occasionally came out into the room. It was easy. It wasn't like having extra dogs; it was more like having guinea pigs.

As they grew, their distinct personalities emerged, and wouldn't you know it? Although I wasn't supposed to, I had fallen for the female, the one we weren't keeping. She was so incredibly sweet that she had charmed me, but I kept it to myself. It was absolutely impossible to consider having four dogs in a New York City apartment. I started to talk to Matthew about adopting Wisteria. I felt like I could manage losing her if she stayed in the family.

Matt's wife, Lara, definitely wanted her, but Matt remained harder to convince. Then Lara and Pixie, Matt's three-year-old daughter, came to New York City for a visit. I gave Wisteria to Pixie to hold and she loved her; I captured the moment on digital film and e-mailed it to Matt. "Say no to this!" I wrote. I felt him beginning to come around, though I was careful not to mention anything to Pixie about it. Violet brought it up, though, since she thought it was a good idea.

Meanwhile, Paul was discussing Wisteria's potential adoption with his brother, uncle, and best friend, Mike. There were a lot of people who wanted her, and that was before they even saw her picture.

I e-mailed Paul after getting off the phone with Matt.

Julie: "I think Matt is going to take Wisteria!"

Paul: "Great! Did you send him the picture of Pixie holding her?"

Julie: "Yes, he thought it was adorable!!"

Paul: "Of course!"

Julie: "It's perfect!"

Five minutes passed and I wrote back to him again.

Julie: "Except, now I want to keep her."

Paul: "Me too."

Julie: "Really? I am so happy! So we're keeping her?"

Paul: "I guess we are."

Julie: *"Yay!!!!!!!!!"*

Paul: "We do what we feel is right, but we don't always do what's best for us."

So we took Wisteria off the market and we let everyone know. It just seemed impossible to break up the puppies, no matter what anyone said. They were two peas in a pod! They slept huddled together, and when Wisteria got a little adventurous and went out of the box, Fiorello wept for her to return and vice versa. All of the breeder and veterinary people told us that this didn't mean anything. They would do perfectly fine apart; it happened all the time. Dahlia was a doting mother, they said, but as soon as she finished nursing she'd be kickin' them to the curb. I didn't disbelieve this, but I felt like our situation was different. Our mother dog was different, and our puppies were different. She may have had to say good-bye to her children before, but she wouldn't have to now. She had a home, and she should be able to keep her children there with her.

Just like when you have a baby, when you get used to one phase of puppy development, suddenly everything changes. I thought they'd live in that UPS box forever, but one day they were just done with it. They didn't want to go in it again for any reason. Dahlia was ready to roam the house as well, and the puppies had some serious exploring to do, since among Paul, Violet, and me, there were plenty of shoes that were just begging to be chewed up.

We kept them in the pen at night and when we went out, but the rest of the time they had free rein. Dahlia would try to get away from them more and more, but not totally. They had started to eat little puppy meals, but they still nursed when they wanted to, sharp teeth and all. And Dahlia withstood it. Everyone said she would let them know when she was finished having them suckle, but she never did. Eventually they weaned themselves, but she still assiduously minded them, even when they were pretty much done nursing. Sometimes I thought she was through with them and then I'd see her giving them a full inner-ear bath and nuzzling their tummies.

When they were big enough, they slept with her on the couch, one tucked into her front paws and the other nestled into her stomach. If she got up, they glommed together, but when she came back they returned to position.

Four dogs. *Four dogs. Cuatro perros. Quatre chiens. Fir hunten. Vier honden. Vier Hunde, fire hunde, quattro cani, quatro cães, yonhiki inu ken, mbwa nne, Arbaa klavim, keturi suniai, tesseres skeeli, char kutte, négy kutyá, chetiri sobaki.* It sounds crazy in any language, doesn't it? It's quite something to wrap your head around—you have one dog and then it's four. Like you're a size small one day and the next you're XXXL. You have one head—then four. One apple, then an orchard. One goldfish, then a herd of elephants.

We were starting to get it. We were not getting comfortable with it, but getting used to it. I was talking to a new friend of mine, Deb, whom I had met recently at a book festival in San Jose. It was one of those cosmic meetings where you find a person and the way they look and sound is so familiar that you keep trying to figure out how you must know them. Within five minutes, we discovered we had one very close friend in common and lived five blocks from each other on the Upper West Side, where we both had kids and husbands named Paul. We had that immediate openness that you sometimes feel when you meet a friend in a strange land. I found out she was going through a very hard time; her beloved father had been recently diagnosed with cancer and it was just a harsh, swift blow. He had only a matter of months to live.

Right before Thanksgiving, I ran into Deb when she was walking Lucas, her cute little Havanese puppy. She was filling me in on the stuff with her dad and I was trying to figure out if there was anything I could do. As it turned out, they were going to Delaware and someone in the house where they were staying was allergic to dogs. They would be away for only a few days, and I happily offered to keep Lucas. It was one thing I was completely capable of handling.

So for a few days we had five dogs, and only one of them, Bea, was housebroken. Dahlia's birth had left her incontinent, and everyone else was still learning. It was like living in a giant litter box. I walked Dahlia and Bea with Lucas and thought, This is only three dogs; I will be walking four.

A few weeks later Deb's father passed away, and we took Lucas in for a week. I was heartbroken for Deb and her family, and it was a blessing to actually be able to help them.

When Lucas left, we went back to having "just" four dogs. It was like that old story about the guy complaining that his house is too small and the town elder keeps telling him to move his cows, then his sheep, then his chickens, then his horses into the house and finally when he can't stand it anymore the town elder tells him to move them back out and suddenly his house seems huge. Well, it was almost like that.

It was overwhelming, but we were still not even taking the puppies outside—and that future prospect just hung over me like a roof of dread. When the day finally came that their inoculations were complete and they were ready to go out for walks, I delayed it some more. It was still winter, and cold and windy when I'd taken them to the vet. They had been so terrified to be out of the apartment that we decided it would be better to wait until the weather improved. Sun and warmth would be so much more welcoming. In the meantime, they were paper trained and really pretty good! I thought about the crazy, unsocialized puppies of John, the man in Washington Heights. Our puppies were lovely! They had also grown into their own personalities. Wisteria was what you'd call "mouthy." She was a biter, but Fiorello was as gentle as a lamb. He never bit, though he started to pee on everything, which Wisteria never did.

They had such a funny relationship. Sometimes I'd open the front door in the morning to get the paper, and they'd amble into the hallway.

"Okay, come back in," I'd say, and Wisteria would, but Fiorello would keep sniffing around. So Wisteria would go into the hall and wrangle him into the apartment. We were endlessly correcting Wisteria's teething on us. "No biting! Wisteria, no biting!" She didn't really stop, but Fiorello would start yelling at her—he had a real voice, gruff and growly like an angry bear in a tiny puppy cave mixed with

Billy Bob Thornton in *Sling Blade,* and he would lecture her—"Rururrruu RuRuRuRruururururRURURURURU urrrrr"—until she was a huddled, apologetic mass.

Puppies are constantly inventing new ways to be bad. It's fascinating. You come into a room they've been in and see pieces of debris and try to figure out what you had that was made from wicker or what had been stuffed with fluff. Violet would regrettably leave her bin of dolls open and the puppies would systematically eat the hands and feet off of all of them. They would not swallow them; they would just bite them off and leave them around like Hawkeye's *M*A*S*H* nightmare. One morning I walked into the living room and found Violet's finely crafted *Wizard of Oz* pop-up book open on the floor. The puppies had eaten the whole tornado. It was now a very different story.

The first springlike day was a Saturday. Paul was home, so we decided to take everyone outside. We got ready to take the puppies out for their first walk. We put new batteries in the camera and spent an absurd amount of time getting all the dogs' halters on. I remembered from Beatrice's puppyhood that being good on a leash is not an innate trait. It takes time to learn. But when I taught her to behave on a leash, she was one puppy, and I lived right by a park. Now we were taking out two adult dogs and two puppies, and it was on crazy Broadway, where, more often than not, there were loud noises and traffic. A bus stop was just in front of our building, and frequently the sitting bus would emit this loud exhalation sound. The puppies just might be a little frightened. Well, in reality they were flat-out petrified. Fiorello glued himself in between my feet, like he was in an armored ankle car, and shook. Wisteria sobbed. Though Paul, Violet, and I were walking the four of them, somehow three people just weren't enough for four dogs. Not by a long shot. It seemed like we would need two people per dog. Ultimately I carried Fiorello, while Wisteria steeled herself to persevere.

After that, Fiorello refused to go on walks. When he heard the leashes rattling he would hide under the bed. I didn't want to push him, and I wasn't dying to walk four dogs, so I just took Wisteria with Bea and Dahlia. Wisteria liked it a lot and found the whole experience to be great fun; she just didn't understand she was supposed to go to the bathroom outside. We'd take these long walks and she'd trot in and head for the newspaper to relieve herself. Curiosity ultimately got the best of Fiorello, and he would start coming out to watch us get ready to go and then he would allow a harness to be put on him. Before I knew it, he was going out, too.

He went from being a timid hider to being the chief bigmouth pain in the ass, barking and barking and barking his brains out anytime we passed another dog. He was a total embarrassment.

Paul walked the four dogs a couple of times, but then he didn't want to anymore. He would come in and say, "I hate having four dogs," as if I had sneaked them in under my coat. He called Dahlia the Trojan Dog. She was falling slightly out of favor because she had gone from being a loving mother to a crotchety old dog, at times really aggressive. She bit all of us and attacked Bea daily. I still knew there was no way I could let her go to another home. I just couldn't do it to her. When she was lying quietly on the couch, my heart broke for her, but when I passed by her in what she considered a too abrupt fashion, she'd lash out and chomp on my leg. "I hate you!" I'd shout. And then she'd look at me with her soft brown eyes and I knew she hadn't meant it. Every time she fought with Bea, which was more and more often, additional teeth fell out. (One night Paul thought she had cottage cheese on her lip—but it was a tooth.) So technically speaking, the bites shouldn't have hurt that much, but her remaining choppers were fierce weapons. It was an unhappy situation in our house and I was to blame. The dog thing had been my idea. One morning Paul woke up and stepped into a dump in bare feet. "Next time," he said, glaring at me, "you should rescue cakes."

Mostly, it was just me walking them. My own private Iditarod. And it wasn't a picnic. Just so you know, if you ever see a person walking four dogs, there are two things you can cross off your list of what to exclaim: (1) "Who's walking who?"

and (2) "Looks like you got your hands full." Both lines are stupid and someone else has already said them. You might consider saying, "Hey, pretty girl!" or "Wow, four dogs sure make you look thin!"

This was what happened when we went out:

1) I pick up and untangle the leashes that are all woven together like a macramé plant hanger.
2) Wisteria bites, bites, bites my hands and runs around crazily (*"Mom, Wisteria has sticking-out teeth, like a bear!"*), then she bites a hole in my sweatpants.
3) Fiorello BARKS, BARKS, BARKS in case anyone might forget to take him.
4) Beatrice shivers, anxious that somehow she's going to be hurt.
5) Dahlia stays in her bed waiting for an engraved invitation.
6) I tell (a) Wisteria to stop biting, (b) Fiorello to stop barking, (c) Dahlia to get over here, and (d) Bea to relax.
7) We finally get everyone leashed up and they nearly take my arm out of the socket lunging into the hall.
8) The elevator finally comes, and since we're on the sixteenth floor, it stops for other people to get on; the people look at us grimly and say they'll wait for the next one.

9) We arrive at the lobby and one of the dogs decides it's close enough to the outside and pees or poops on the floor. The doormen glare at me.
10) We go outside, and I can see an elderly man with his two Lab mixes coming down the street. One is as old as Methuselah, blind and deaf. He looks like Balto compared to his companion, who is in one of those doggie wheelchairs. I take my pack of a-holes in the other direction because I know they want to rumble with the Geriatric Gang.
11) My cell phone rings, and even though it's Barack Obama asking me to dinner at the White House, I just can't get to it in time.
12) They all poop in unison (except Wisteria, who will wait until we get back into the apartment), but my baggies fly out of my pocket into the wind. I run after the bags and get them and then I can't remember where the pile is so I walk around like I've lost a diamond stud till I'm able to find the "present."
13) We walk farther. Fiorello yells at everyone, and Wisteria still refuses to use the outside when there's a perfectly good newspaper waiting in Violet's room.
14) People point at us, occasionally wanting a picture, occasionally telling me that the puppies are in fact (a) Aztec Chihuahuas or (b) Ibizan hounds.

15) We turn around and the process happens in reverse.
16) I am awarded the Medal of Valor for all that I've done (in my dreams).
17) A few hours later I do it again.

I have a theory about my dogs' behavior issues. It's that saying "All dogs go to heaven." They hear it all the time. Why bother curbing yourself if you have this Get Out of Hell Free card?

In between those times there are a lot of laughs. Paul, Violet, and I sing songs about the dogs like, "Wisteria has bigger ears than any doggie should; Wisteria is prettier than an old block of wood" to the tune of "Born Free." I yell at the dogs in a Carmela Soprano voice, "Dahlia Marie, get ya little ass down heah!" We give the dogs full names—Fiorello Luigi Parmegiana and Wisteria Louis-Dreyfus (sometimes Wisteria Louise Johnson and sometimes I can't deal with the mouthful that is Wisteria so I call her Francine)—and we announce their entrance into the debutante ball in our living room.

Violet treated Wisteria like a sibling. There were days when she would say she hated Wisteria and others when she couldn't wait to torment her. But Fiorello was the love of her life. She carried him around awkwardly from a cozy spot on the couch to sit on her lap in the bathroom while she went. Whatever he did, she had a good explanation.

Me: "Fiorello peed on the bedspread!"

Violet: "He doesn't like the flowered pattern."

Me: "Fiorello peed on my jeans."

Violet: "They shouldn't be on the floor, Mom."

Me: "Fiorello peed on the bath mat."

Violet: "What a good boy! He knew to go to the bathroom in the bathroom."

Violet is a true dog person. She doesn't mind being licked on the mouth or jumped on. She thinks about the dogs' feelings and tells me that when she grows up, along with being an artist, she's going to rescue puppies, too. I explain to her that she already is.

At other times, I'm breaking up fights between Bea and Dahlia and always getting bitten. I tell my friend Robin that as much as I love them, the four dogs are getting impossible. Dahlia had become flagrantly incontinent, regularly walking up and taking a giant pee by my feet. It was a lot and even I was getting tired of our apartment smelling like the corridors of the Union Square subway station. Robin told me about how she had two old dogs, a male and a female. The female couldn't stand to be away from the male so Robin, an Emmy Award–winning TV writer, sat her down one day and said, "Listen, I want you to know that if he dies, you're going to have to die, too." The next day, the female was standing in the living room and she looked at Robin, took a breath, and keeled over onto the floor, two X's in her eyes. It was good to have someone to laugh about it all with.

When Dahlia's puppies hit eight months, she still licked their ears and nuzzled them. She yelled at them for being annoying, but she was never, ever aggressive toward them. She was still a wonderful mother, and for that alone I had to love her.

Paul and I had the discussion on a daily basis. Four dogs are too many. What are we going to do? Let's let my brother have Wisteria. We can't. Let's let Uncle Dan take Beatrice. We can't. Let's find a new home through Petfinder and try to place Dahlia and one of her puppies. We can't. There wasn't a solution. The best I could do was keep talking about possibilities. I hoped that my parents might take one (or two), but my father didn't want them because he likes fuzzy dogs whose coats suit his winter sporting habit. We continued to discuss future maybes, but in the end, we just couldn't let any one of them go.

I have a saying: "In every life a little dog you don't want must fall, and that's probably going to be the one that buries you."

These puppies, whom we'll probably call "the puppies" until they're fifteen, chew our shoes and piss up our rugs; when you yell, "No!" at them, they wiggle around like you just told them they hit the lotto. And it's messy, very messy, but it's miraculous. And if I get up to go to the bathroom at 4 A.M. or come home at four in the afternoon, they're as happy to see me as if I just came back from a tour of Vietnam.

One week, Dahlia and Beatrice got into a bad scuffle. For the first time in a long time, Dahlia was the one who got hurt. A gash in her leg. Fiorello, now fully grown, sat beside her, licking her wound and tending to her like a good Italian son.

Wisteria became my shadow. Wherever I went, she was right behind me, and then she insisted I take her into bed at night. When the same thing happened with Violet, I realized it was simpler to cave in and let her sleep with us than spend nights going back and forth with her. I'm of the same mind with the little black dog. I remember the point when Otto stopped sleeping with me. One day he just didn't have the energy to hop up. I relish the warm dog by my feet, and feel like if she wants to be near me that badly, I should let her.

One night I got into bed alone. Then Wisteria came up, and Bea came up and Violet jumped in and Paul got in. And Violet went to get Fiorello, though he only stayed for a minute because he wanted to go back to his mother.

"There are too many heartbeats in this bed!" Paul said. "We've got to do something about this."

And Wisteria jumped up and started furiously licking him and I realized that was the answer I should have been giving him all along.

WE SPENT THE FOLLOWING summer taking trips with the dogs to the beach and my parents' house. It was an exceptionally lovely summer, perfect weather and lots of fun visits with family.

Toward the end of August, Violet and I went to my parents' house, and Paul stayed in Manhattan to work. The first day there, Dahlia seemed uncomfortable to me. I planned to take her to the vet, but I had an idea that it wasn't any one thing. I spoke to Sheryl on the phone, and we both thought that having the puppies had just taken too much of a toll on her poor body. I sat down next to her on the couch and petted her and kissed her and she fell asleep. We lost Dahlia the next day.

It was one day short of her one-year anniversary with us. Though it had been probably the most intensely hard on her physically, I also believed it was the best year of her life. She had her puppies and got to keep them and she knew they were safe.

Walking through my parents' fields of wildflowers, I explained to Violet what happened, emphasizing that Dahlia was quite old. Once again we were talking about heaven. Violet was so very sad, most upset at the idea that the puppies were now orphaned. They'd never had a dad and now their mom was gone. When I suggested to her that Paul and I could be their mommy and daddy, too, she was profoundly relieved. I think I was as well.

In that amazing way that kids do, she started elaborating on the images I'd given her of heaven—not the heaven I imagine now, but the one I believed in as a kid. She named all the people we'd lost who would be waiting for Dahlia there: Grandpa Roger and Baba Jean and Uncle Ernest and Aunt Phyllis and Aunt Susie and Aunt Iris and Otto and Moses. Dahlia would be healthy and not old and have anything she wanted to eat and all the toys she wanted to play with and the days would all be bright and warm. "Oh!" she said, remembering, "and Dahlia can have all of her teeth again!"

By the time we headed back to the house, the sun was setting. The clouds were the colors of the inside of a peach. I held Violet's hand and I think we both felt some peace thinking of Dahlia up there in heaven.

LESSON ELEVEN

How to Find the Right Fit

If you're going to P. Diddy's clambake on the North Fork of Long Island and you need to know whether a Pinot Blanc or a Riesling works better with Montauk clams, you could consult with my friend Jessica. If you want to know which toaster oven will leave the smallest carbon footprint, talk to my dad. If you're thinking of traveling to an exotic, yet comfy, locale and need a recommendation, ask my friend Jancee. And if anybody has a dog question, they come to me. You know, like: *I have a dog and it's sick/not housebroken/biting people. I want to get a dog, what kind? My neighbor's dog never stops barking; can I write them an anonymous note? I found a stray dog; what do I do? Do you think the Monster of Montauk is a bulldog? Etc.* . . . I have the distinct honor of being known by friends, fans, followers, and family as the dog expert, to my face anyway. Behind my back it's the dog nut.

For over a year, a friend of mine, Andrea, has been asking if we could get together and talk about dogs. She has three children and they desperately want a dog. She had a brief, unsuccessful adoption of a mutt from a shelter, and she doesn't want to make another mistake. She's essentially starting from zero, as in, she didn't have dogs growing up, she's not a woman who stops to pet every dog on the street, she's really not a dog person. We make a date for Violet and me to come over. Our daughters will play Polly Pockets and we will chat canines.

Her building on Riverside Drive is one of those grand, elegant prewar buildings that you imagine Katharine Hepburn stepping out of to hail a Checker Cab.

Past the doorman and the elevator attendant, we get to Andrea's and she ushers us in with warmth and affection. Right away I notice the distinct lack of smells. The next thing that catches my attention is that there are no pee-soaked newspapers on her hardwood floors. It's tidy and photogenic. I make Violet take off her boots; I take off my sneakers and we go inside.

Andrea gestures for me to come and sit on the creamy suede couch, whose legs are suspiciously without bite marks, the fabric free of tears from tiny teeth and nails. There's an oriental rug without faded yellow stains; lovely art and sculptures sit undisturbed. Beneath the glass coffee table, there are no chewed orthotics or Dora the Explorer toys bitten in half like an extra in *Jaws*. The last detail I take in is Andrea's pants—clean and dazzlingly white. The apartment whispers to me, *"Dogs do not live here."*

I sit carefully on the couch facing the view of the river and think about the similarities between Andrea's and my homes. Well, we both have walls and floors and ceilings.

"So!" she says. "I don't even know where to begin."

"That's fine," I assure her. "I didn't know anything before I got Otto. Why don't you describe for me your ideal dog."

The thing is, Andrea's not really the one dreaming of the dog. Her children are, mainly her nine-year-old son.

"Well," she says slowly, "the problem with the dog we adopted was it had very bad emotional problems, like severe separation anxiety. . . . We were totally ill-equipped."

"I understand," I say. "I understand," I say again. "That's totally . . . understandable."

We talk a little more about the dog who didn't work out, with me understanding, and then she tries to put into words what she wants. "Not terribly needy." Her husband travels frequently for work and her children are in different schools. Then she adds, "Not high maintenance."

I start talking about good apartment dogs.

"I don't want a very small dog, like a Chihuahua," she says, wrinkling her nose. I nod. "Not too small and yappy. But not too big." She holds her hand about three feet above the ground. "Like maybe this big?"

"Uh-huh." I nod. I am thinking of the perfect dog. Martha. From the children's book *Martha Speaks*.

"Not a dog who barks a lot." She pauses and then blurts, "I don't want to sound awful saying this, but you know how some dogs smell?" At the word "smell," she seems to recall a very foul dog-related odor.

"Yeah," I laugh, "I don't think you sound awful." I really don't. I see how much Andrea just doesn't really want a dog, but her kids do, and she loves them and wants them to be happy. She's being as honest as she can be so she doesn't end up with another situation that doesn't work and hurts her family.

"In terms of smell, I think there are some dogs that are smellier than others," I say, clinically. "I also think all dogs have some smell."

Andrea looks worried.

"Though," I say quickly, "my aunt Mattie's basset hound, Norman, smelled like cigarettes and my aunt Phyllis's poodle smelled like Estée Lauder's Youth Dew." I stop. "Poodles are great!"

"I don't want a poodle. I don't want a *poofy* dog," she says.

"Well, not all poodles smell like Youth Dew and they aren't all poofy either. It's how people decide to cut the hair. You know, go to the groomer and ask for a Continental cut or whatever with the pom-poms?" I go into my poodle rap. "We had a standard poodle growing up. She was called Misty because she was gray. She just had evenly cut hair—well, not so even because my dad did it in our basement. . . ." She wasn't convinced. "Poodles are very smart, and they don't shed."

"Oh!" she says, remembering. She shakes her head no as she says, "I can't have a dog who sheds."

"Boston terriers don't shed," I say, putting in a quick plug for the home team.

"What about French bulldogs?" she asks.

"They shed more than Bostons, and I think they tend to have more health problems. A lot of them suffer from joint diseases and spinal disorders." I do love French bulldogs, but I think they're a breed for a more experienced dog owner.

Being a dog person is not something you can force. Sometimes I watch people who want to be seen as dog people, but they really aren't. They pet and scratch a dog with a manic intensity. "Here's the spot!" they say as the dog seizes up, twitching, looking more bothered than anything, like it might succumb to shaken dog syndrome. After they've made sure everyone has seen them petting the dog, they sneak off to bathe in Purell.

We speak further and I suggest that Andrea look at dogs when she's walking around and if she sees one she likes, find out what it is and then we can investigate the possibilities together. As she walks me to the door, she asks if I know about golden doodles or Labradoodles or cockapoos or Portuguese water dogs. I honestly don't, but I suggest she get a basic dog book that breaks down the breeds and characteristics.

We leave and I think about my knowledge. So much of what I know about dogs, like what I know about trees and birds, I learned listening to my father. Chows are mean, Jack Russells are a friggin' pain in the neck, beagles howl, terriers roam, golden retrievers are gentle and sweet. But I then rolled that information into my experience and have come to the conclusion that every dog is unique. There are absolutely dogs who are true to breed in their traits, whether it be stubbornness or mouthiness or gentleness. But I've known hyper and mellow boxers, sweet and vicious German shepherds. It depends on the dog, where it came from, who bred it, how it was raised and socialized. And though a howling beagle might drive my father crazy, there are events where people with beagles get together with their dogs for a massive howlelujah chorus.

I am always interested in what brings a kind of dog to a certain person. It's like when you see a really odd couple—like James Carville and Mary Matalin—and you try to figure out what attracted them to each other. With dogs, it's pure. You never find a person who chose a dog because it has a trust fund or an endorsement deal with Nike.

Unsurprisingly, the people who like Boston terriers often go for French bulldogs, too, and the whole flat-faced line. I do love all dogs, although some breeds, I must confess, I just don't get. I never understood the appeal of Chesapeake Bay retrievers; to me they appear decidedly uncuddly, like they're made out of wet clay, like Weimaraners. Pulis, with their mountains of matted dreadlocks, are also not attractive to me, nor are clumber spaniels with their Omar Sharif eyes. Believe me, this isn't a judgment; they're just not my type. I know some people may not think Boston terriers are beautiful. Some men don't like women with long hair; some men don't like women. I don't choose dogs with protruding noses (though the two of them running around my apartment don't know that). And for the most part I don't go for big dogs, though I do love Great Danes. I always wanted to have a Great Dane just for the odd image of me walking it with a Boston terrier. I'd glare at anyone who stared at us and yell a crazy, *"What are you looking at?"* And actually, it isn't that I don't go for big dogs as much as I don't want one sleeping in my bed, and that is where they'd always end up.

Certain dogs are better suited for different lifestyles. People who fly a lot and bring their pets along need them to be under twenty pounds to fit in a carrier under their airline seat. That's a real consideration.

If you've got allergies, it wouldn't be smart to choose a triple-coated breed, like German shepherds. In New York City, certain stores don't allow dogs, but if you carry them, it's okay. I could not manage that if I had a rottweiler.

I feel very strongly that people shouldn't choose a breed that resembles them. The goal should not be to potentially end up in the local newspaper contest of people who look like their dogs. Though I understand that that may be unavoidable. I was once in a bodega with Otto reaching for something on a high shelf. Behind me I heard a woman say in a heart-stopping voice, "Oh my God—that dog is breathtakingly beautiful!" I looked at her; she was Otto in a blond wig.

Mastiffs, the dogs I grew up with, were chosen by my parents, and though they had very big noses and reddish blond hair like my dad, I don't think he picked them for their familial resemblance. They were sort of big English country manor dogs, and we had a large house and lots of land . . . and sometimes my mother made Yorkshire pudding. The main thing was the dogs were the right scale for our home.

Sounds kind, right? Giving that big dog all that room to roam. Except our dogs always stayed with us in the kitchen. They'd pour their bodies into the tightest corner or the narrowest space between two counters so you'd have to vault over them to get by. This is one of the reasons I tell people I don't feel bad about big dogs in the city. Our humongous mastiffs had a giant house and acres to roam. They'd go from the kitchen floor to lying on a small spot of grass outside the kitchen door. They didn't ramble through the fields; they snoozed. Urban people tend to compensate for the space by giving their dogs lots of park exercise and the dog runs. My small city dogs do more with me than my Katonah dogs ever did (or wanted to do).

At night the dogs would sleep in my brother Matt's room. He was the animal kid. His long body would be smashed against the wall by Lioness or Reggie, the largest of our mastiffs (weighing in at a lithe 160 pounds), who slept on his side, legs splayed, giant head on his pillow, managing to utilize more of the bed real estate than Matt ever could. It's a thing about sleeping with dogs I've noticed over the years that is similar to sleeping with children; you can move them to a spot that's better for you a million times, but they always spring back to where they were like a bungee cord off a bridge. Matt once broke up a fight between Lioness and a newer mastiff puppy, Thumper. They'd gone at it a couple of times, and this time it was when Matt was alone in the kitchen, having just come in from feeding the horses. Breaking up a fight is not a good thing to do, but I've also done it. As much as you know you shouldn't, sometimes you can't help it. And Matt's arm got severely chomped and he needed a bunch of stitches. He still has the bite marks today.

It was definitely a Katonah thing, the multitude of big dogs. Like a Ralph Lauren ad, the picture wasn't complete without the oversized, khaki- and sienna-colored canines. I remember sitting at our pool watching Reggie, the largest mastiff we had, lying down beside our chaise longue in the sun, his long tongue lolling out every so often to lick up some ants. Mastiffs also have a unique type of drool, dense and hanging in long curtains from their little black lips, usually containing particles of dirt or leaves or, if they've been lying on my floor, a sequin or a sparkle. But the massiveness of the dogs was sort of specific to the country life. I always appreciated my friend Barbara. She'd come over to my house and yell, "Get them away from me!" At least she was honest.

My relationship with our dogs was strained as a kid. Mastiffs have triple coats and shed in sandy clumps of hair tumbleweeds. I unfortunately had asthma and allergies, so much of my connection to them happened from a distance. If I would pet one, my eyes would water and my nose would tickle. Yet I still had great love for them even from afar. Not unlike my crush on Timothy Hutton. Lioness was the dog I'd known the longest. We got her when I was four, right before we moved to Katonah. She had the most Nana-like personality; my father often told stories of how she watched us kids in the pool or followed us on sleigh-riding trips.

On the opposite end of the size spectrum, we had an odd-looking cairn terrier mix. We got her because a friend's cairn had been "knocked up" by something long and flat, and they had free puppies. It was one of those oh-what-the-heck things. Her name was Meatball. My brother Matt rechristened her "Peenie," like he did with every dog we had—none of them went by their Christian names; they all had their "Matthew names" (Lioness and Reggie were both called "Hoady"; Misty was called "Mewdance") and those seemed to win.

Peenie had a wise, Yoda-like quality. My grandmother said she was horrible-looking and called her "the broom dog." She did have some very strange hair, kind of matted but thick and coarse like a Before picture in a shampoo ad. She always had sticks and prickers from the yard attached to her, and she'd regularly saunter into the house with a branch attached to her leg. My aunt Phyllis defended her, calling her "the elegant dog." She had the immovable grace and dignity found in

African herd animals like elk and wildebeests, even after she frequently and tragically got skunked. We watched her turn every new dog that came into our homes into her apprentice. She would teach them to behave, to not be afraid, and to roll in dead things. Upon turning fifteen, Peenie started to show her age. She didn't go for long walks and she'd sit in the sand by my parents' pond for the whole day. My mother talked about the end coming and we all worried about how it would go, but she kept on month after month and year after year. One November morning, my mother let her out and watched her from the window. She went not to the rolling grasses in front of the house like she normally did, but to a wooded area, filled with briars, not trails. Creeping under an expansive raspberry bramble, she disappeared, nobly going off to die alone.

No one would have ever looked at her and thought, She is going to be the best dog you ever have. And more often than not, you don't end up getting the dog that you want. You get the dog that you need.

From Otto, who showed me I could be in a reciprocal nurturing relationship, to Dahlia, who proved that life continues to surprise (and that you can drop the jaw on the most jaded New Yorker when your senior bitch gives birth), each dog in my life has brought me something or taught me a lesson that improved the quality of my life. I am richer in every way because of the dogs I've known.

A week before Thanksgiving, Paul's uncle, a scholar and collector of antiquities, passed away. He was twice divorced, with no children and no pets. An isolated misanthrope, but one who was always delighted to see Otto and later Beatrice. He left behind a rent-controlled seven-room apartment on West End Avenue (two blocks from our apartment though we'd never been inside) overflowing with his collections—hundreds of paintings, books, militaria, ephemera, coins, pretty much anything you've ever seen at an auction or flea market. (Think Collyer brother.) Due in part to his poor health over the last several years, the majority of his purchases remained in their original packaging. Paintings wrapped in brown paper and twine, postcards in bags, a dozen sabers under the couch hidden by crumpled-up newspapers. It fell to Paul and his brothers (and wives) to do the excavating. The first day Violet and I came and helped, but between the dust and the impenetrable clutter, it was impossible for us to stay too long. Besides, we needed to walk the dogs.

We went home and picked them up and headed toward the park. On Riverside we passed a man in his sixties who from his stance I recognized as "not a dog lover." Violet and I pulled the dogs over to the side so he could pass, but not before he looked me in the eye, motioned to my pack, and said with great irritation, "What is the point?"

I ignored him, and Violet and I kept walking. "Mom, why didn't you answer him?"

That's the thing about kids: they're constantly forcing you into "teachable moments." I turned around, and the man was still glaring. I said, "Well, the National Institutes of Health has proven that owning pets has significant health benefits including the boosting of survival rates for coronary care patients. Dog ownership promotes regular exercise, being near a dog lowers its owner's blood pressure, and when a person interacts with a dog, the central nervous system releases several hormones that cause feelings of pleasure—included in that is oxytocin."

Mr. Cranky brushed me off, but Violet was very happy I defended our herd.

Later I told the story to Paul, who was sitting on the couch with the dogs. He asked me not to talk to crazies anymore and then started interviewing the dogs in his William F. Buckley accent. He took turns asking each of them, "What *is* your *point*?"

The dogs tend to get very excited when they're being interviewed. So they were jumping, wiggling, yipping, and grabbing toys and dropping them on Paul's lap. Fiorello got so excited, he peed a little. Violet and I were laughing hysterically. Their point, it seemed to all of us, was pretty evident.

Acknowledgments

Even though she's a cat person, I am down on my knees with gratitude to my dear friend and agent, Esther Newberg. There would just be nothing without her. Standing ovation for Megan Lynch, my editor, whose brilliance and good grooming could stand up to any poodle anytime! Huzzahs to Geoff Kloske, captain of the Riverhead Dream Team (RIV-ER-HEAD! RIV-ER-HEAD!). Enormous thanks to Mih-ho Cha for her unimaginable smarts and endless kindness, and to everyone else at Riverhead Books.

Rainbows, unicorns, and hearts to Barbara Warnke, Jancee Dunn, Gigi Levangie Grazer, Lizzie Skurnick, Margaret Fox, Kristin Moavenian, Sadie Resnick, Mandi Zuckerman, Molly Jong-Fast, Amy Harmon, Brenda Copeland, Kate Christensen, Patty Marx, Ken Foster, Deborah Copaken Kogan, Hyatt Bass, Martha Broderick, Diane Sokolow, Sam Sokolow, Robin Green, Joy Riley, Sheryl Trent, Northeast Boston Terrier Rescue, Lynda Barry, Emma Straub, John

T. Smith, John Lewis, Elisabeth Albert, Arthur Einstein, Arthur Phillips, Leslie Verbitsky, Megan Gliebe, Jen Maxwell, Ann Binstock, Haley Fox, Susan Roxborough, Wendy Hammond, Claudia Glaser-Mussen, Abby Weintraub, Nicole Leibman, David Rakoff, Rich Cohen, Jessica Medoff, Dan Menaker, Patrick Brown, Bethanne Patrick, Erin McHugh, Kimberly Burns, Marian Brown, Carrie Fisher, Victoria Comella, Sarah Bowlin, Kari Stuart, Mattie Matthews (the savior to my dogs), and my brother Brian for coming up with the title.

All the luff in the world to my family (especially my sweet baby Violet Jean) and to all of the people who rescue animals.

The bestselling memoirist shows how saving a dog can sometimes help you save yourself.

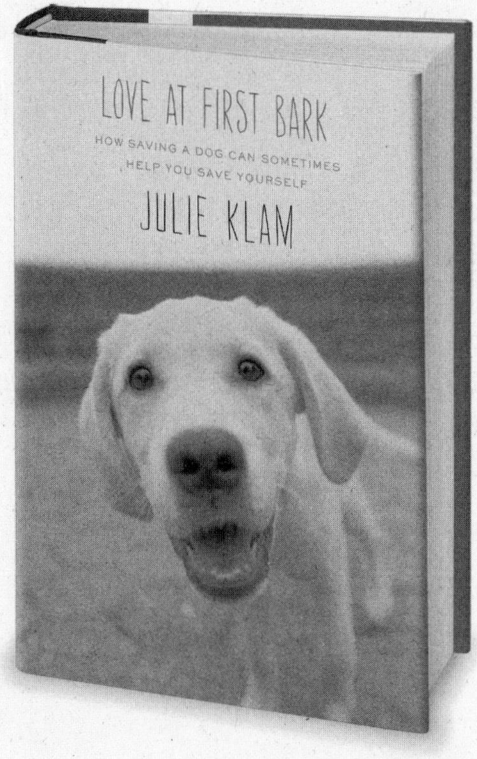

"Julie Klam is like Proust, if he wrote about dogs instead of madeleines, wrote in English instead of French, had better hair—and wrote exceptionally hilarious books that you can't help reading all at once."

—PATRICIA MARX

RIVERHEAD BOOKS
A member of Penguin Group (USA) Inc.
RiverheadBooks.com • facebook.com/RiverheadBooks
JulieKlam.com • facebook.com/JulieKlamAuthor

T161.0611